T0059101

G. SCHIRMER'S COLLECTION OF OPERA LIBRETTOS

GÖTTERDÄMMERUNG

Music Drama in Three Acts (five scenes) and Prologue
(From the trilogy DER RING DES NIBELUNGEN)

by

Richard Wagner

English Version by
STEWART ROBB

Ed. 2516

G. SCHIRMER, Inc.

DISTRIBUTED BY

HAL•LEONARD®
CORPORATION

7777 W. BLUEMOUND RD. P.O. BOX 13819 MILWAUKEE, WI 53213

Important Notice

Performances of this opera must be licensed by the publisher.

All rights of any kind with respect to this opera and any parts thereof, including but not limited to stage, radio, television, motion picture, mechanical reproduction, translation, printing, and selling are strictly reserved.

License to perform this work, in whole or in part, whether with instrumental or keyboard accompaniment, must be secured in writing from the Publisher. Terms will be quoted upon request.

Copying of either separate parts or the whole of this work, by hand or by any other process, is unlawful and punishable under the provisions of the U.S.A. Copyright Act.

The use of any copies, including arrangements and orchestrations, other than those issued by the Publisher, is forbidden.

All inquiries should be directed to the Publisher:

G. Schirmer Rental Department
5 Bellvale Road
Chester, NY 10918
(914) 469-2271

Copyright © 1960 (Renewed) by Stewart Robb
Sole Selling Agent: G. Schirmer, Inc.
International Copyright Secured. All Rights Reserved.
**Warning: Unauthorized reproduction of this publication is
prohibited by Federal law and subject to criminal prosecution.**

GÖTTERDÄMMERUNG

Twenty-six years elapsed between the first draft of the text of Wagner's *Götterdämmerung* and the completion of the score. Since his early days in Dresden Wagner had been deeply interested in the Scandinavian, German and Icelandic sagas that would provide the basic material for his *Ring of the Nibelung*. In 1848 he made his first attempt to put his own dramatic version of the colossal material on paper. It was a poem entitled *Siegfried's Death*. It is to a very large extent identical with the text of what ,we know now as *Götterdämmerung*.

Thus, the last of the four works that form the *Ring* was in fact the first of the texts to be conceived and written by the composer. Soon he realized, that it could not cover the entire story. In 1851 he prefixed *Siegfried's Death* with a second drama, calling it *Young Siegfried*. It was later to become *Siegfried*, the third evening of the cycle. In the following year, he put before it still another poem, *The Valkyrie* and finally *The Rhinegold*, the "Fore-Evening" which is the foundation of the entire *Ring of the Nibelung*. The complete text was printed in 1853 for private distribution.

The music for *The Rhinegold*—as a composer Wagner reversed his method, composing the four works in their proper order—was completed in 1854, *The Valkyrie* in 1856. Both works were performed in Munich in 1869 and 1870. It was not until 1870 that Wagner began to write the music for *Götterdämmerung* in Triebschen, Switzerland. His patron, King Ludwig II of Bavaria, pressed him in vain to finish the score. Wagner, dissatisfied that *The Rhinegold* and *Valkyrie* were performed out of context of the complete Ring, was determined to see *Siegfried* and *Götterdämmerung* performed only as part of a complete performance of the entire cycle, a goal, he knew, he could not see realized until the completion of the Bayreuth Festspielhaus. It was here, during the first season of the new Festival House, on August 17, 1876, that *Götterdämmerung* received its first performance when the entire Ring was performed for the first time under Hans Richter. The cycle was performed three times during this first season at the Festspielhaus, attended by musical notables from all over the world and honored by the presence of Emperor Wilhelm I of Germany and King Ludwig of Bavaria.

The American premiere of *Götterdämmerung* took place at the Metropolitan Opera in New York on January 25, 1888, conducted by Anton Seidl who had been Wagner's assistant in Bayreuth. The scenes of the Norns and Waltraute were omitted in these early performances. Albert Niemann and Lilli Lehmann, both schooled in Bayreuth, sang Siegfried and Brünnhilde and Emil Fischer, a famous Hans Sachs in *Meistersinger*, performed the role of Hagen.

THE STORY

PROLOGUE. On the Valkyries' rock, three Norns spin the rope of Fate, recalling Wotan's days of power and predicting Valhalla's imminent fall. When the rope breaks, they descend in terror to Erda, their mother. At dawn, Siegfried and Brünnhilde emerge from their cave; though fearful that she may lose the hero, she sends him forth to deeds of valor. To remind her of his love, he gives her the ring and, taking her horse Grane in exchange, unites with her in a rapturous farewell.

ACT I. In their castle on the Rhine, Gunther, king of the Gibichungs, and his sister Gutrune, both unwed, ask counsel of their half brother, Hagen. Plotting to secure the ring, Hagen advises Gunther to consolidate his power by marrying Brünnhilde. By means of a magic potion, Siegfried can be induced to forget his bride and win her for Gunther in return for Gutrune's hand. At that very moment the hero's horn announces his approach. Gunther welcomes him, and Gutrune seals his fate by offering him the potion. Hailing Brünnhilde, he drinks and forgets all. Quickly succumbing to Gutrune's beauty, Siegfried agrees to bring Brünnhilde to Gunther. After solemnizing their bargain with an oath to blood-brotherhood, the two men depart. Hagen, keeping watch for their return, gloats over the success of his schemes.

On the Valkyries' rock, Brünnhilde greets Waltraute, who tells her sister that Wotan has warned the gods that their doom is sealed unless Brünnhilde yields the ring to the Rhinemaidens. When she refuses, Waltraute rides off in despair. Dusk falls as Siegfried appears, disguised by the Tarnhelm as Gunther; he wrests the ring from the terrified Brünnhilde and claims her as Gunther's bride.

ACT II. At night, before the Gibichung hall, Alberich forces the sleeping Hagen to swear that he will regain the ring. Siegfried returns, as dawn breaks, with cheerful greetings for Hagen and Gutrune: he has won Brünnhilde for Gunther, who follows shortly. Hagen summons the vassals to welcome the returning king and his bride. When Gunther leads in Brünnhilde, she sees Siegfried and recoils; spying her ring on his finger, she decries the trickery through which she was won, proclaiming Siegfried her true husband. The hero, still under the potion's spell, vows upon Hagen's spear that he has never wronged the woman; snatching the spear point from him, Brünnhilde wrathfully swears that he lies. Siegfried dismisses her charge and then leaves with Gutrune to prepare for their marriage. The dazed Brünnhilde, bent on revenge, reveals to Hagen the hero's one vulnerable spot: a blade in his back will kill him. Taunted by Brünnhilde and lured by Hagen's description of the ring's power, Gunther joins in the murder plot. As the three contemplate the hero's downfall, Siegfried's and Gutrune's wedding procession passes by.

ACT III. Near a mossy bank the three Rhinemaidens bewail their lost treasure. Soon Siegfried approaches, having wandered from his hunting party. The maidens plead for the ring, but he ignores both entreaties and warnings. When the hunting party arrives, Siegfried at Hagen's urging describes his boyhood with Mime, the killing of Fafner and finally—after Hagen gives him a potion to restore his memory—his wooing of Brünnhilde. Pretending indignation, Hagen plunges a spear into his back and stalks off. Hailing Brünnhilde with his last breath, the hero dies; the vassals bear him away on his shield.

At the Gibichung hall, Gutrune nervously awaits her bridegroom's return. Hagen, the first to arrive, tells her that Siegfried has been slain by a wild boar. When his body is carried in, however, the girl accuses Gunther of murder. Hagen admits the crime. Quarreling over possession of the ring, Gunther is killed by Hagen, who falls back in fear from the prize when the dead hero imperiously raises his hand. Brünnhilde, entering majestically, orders a funeral pyre built for Siegfried. Musing on the gods' responsibility for his death, she takes the ring and promises it to the Rhinemaidens. Placing it on her finger, she throws a torch onto the pyre and, joyfully greeting her horse, Grane, rides into the flames. As the river overflows its banks and the hall is consumed, the Rhinemaidens, dragging Hagen to a watery grave, regain their treasure. The flames that engulf Valhalla free the ring of its curse, leaving a human world redeemed by love.

Courtesy of Opera News

CAST OF CHARACTERS

FIRST NORN . . . . Contralto
SECOND NORN . . . . Mezzo-Soprano
THIRD NORN . . . . Soprano
BRÜNNHILDE . . . . Soprano
SIEGFRIED . . . . Tenor
GUNTHER . . . . Baritone
HAGEN . . . . Bass
GUTRUNE . . . . Soprano
WALTRAUTE . . . . Mezzo-Soprano
ALBERICH . . . . Baritone
WOGLINDE . . . . ⎧ ⎫ . . . . . . Soprano
WELLGUNDE . . . . ⎨ Rhinemaidens ⎬ . . . Mezzo-Soprano
FLOSSHILDE . . . . ⎩ ⎭ . . . . Mezzo-Soprano
Vassals and Women.

SYNOPSIS OF SCENES

GÖTTERDÄMMERUNG

VORSPIEL

Auf dem Walkürenfelsen

Die Scene ist dieselbe wie am Schluss des zweiten Tages. Nacht. Aus der Tiefe des Hintergrundes leuchtet Feuerschein auf.

Die drei Nornen, hohe Frauengestalten in langen, dunklen und schleierartigen Faltengewändern. Die Erste (älteste) lagert im Vordergrunde rechts unter der breitästigen Tanne; die Zweite (jüngere) ist an einer Steinbank vor dem Felsengemache hingestreckt; die Dritte (jüngste) sitzt in der Mitte des Hintergrundes auf einem Felsstein des Höhensaumes.

DIE ERSTE NORN
Welch' Licht leuchtet dort?

DIE ZWEITE
Dämmert der Tag schon auf?

DIE DRITTE
Loge's Heer
lodert feurig um den Fels.
Noch ist's Nacht.
Was spinnen und singen wir nicht?

DIE ZWEITE
(zu der ersten)
Wollen wir spinnen und singen,
woran spannst du das Seil?

DIE ERSTE NORN
(erhebt sich, und knüpft während ihres Gesanges ein goldenes Seil mit dem einen Ende an einen Ast der Tanne)
So gut und schlimm es geh'
schling' ich das Seil, und singe.
An der Welt-Esche
wob ich einst,
da gross und stark
dem Stamm entgrünte
weihlicher Aeste Wald.
Im kühlen Schatten
rauscht' ein Quell,
Weisheit raunend
rann sein Gewell';
da sang ich heiligen Sinn.
Ein kühner Gott
trat zum Trunk an den Quell;
seiner Augen eines
zahlt' er als ewigen Zoll.
Von der Welt-Esche
brach da Wotan einen Ast;

eines Speeres Schaft
entschnitt der Starke dem Stamm.
In langer Zeiten Lauf
zehrte die Wunde den Wald;
falb fielen die Blätter,
dürr darbte der Baum;
traurig versiegte
des Quelles Trank:
trüben Sinnes
ward mein Gesang.
Doch web' ich heut'
an der Welt-Esche nicht mehr,
muss mir die Tanne
taugen zu fesseln das Seil:
singe, Schwester,
dir werf' ich's zu:
weisst du, wie das ward?

DIE ZWEITE NORN
(während sie das zugeworfene Seil um einen hervorspringenden Felsstein am Eingange des Gemaches windet)
Treu berat'ner
Verträge Runen
schnitt Wotan
in des Speeres Schaft;
den hielt er als Haft der Welt.
Ein kühner Held
zerhieb im Kampfe den Speer;
in Trümmer sprang
der Verträge heiliger Haft.
Da hiess Wotan
Walhall's Helden
der Welt-Esche
welkes Geäst
mit dem Stamm in Stücke zu fällen:
Die Esche sank;
ewig versiegte der Quell!
Fess'le ich heut'
an den scharfen Fels das Seil,
singe, Schwester,
dir werf' ich's zu:
weisst du, wie das wird?

DIE DRITTE NORN
(das Seil auffangend und dessen Ende hinter sich werfend)
Es ragt die Burg
von Riesen gebaut;
mit der Götter und Helden
heiliger Sippe
sitzt dort Wotan im Saal.

GÖTTERDÄMMERUNG

PRELUDE

The Valkyries' Rock

The same scene as at the end of Siegfried. It is night and from below, at back, gleams the fire.

The three Norns, tall women in somber and flowing drapery, are discovered. The first is crouching under the spreading fir tree; the second is stretched out on a rock before the cave; the third sits on a rock below the peak.

FIRST NORN

What light glimmers there?

SECOND NORN

Is it the dawn so soon?

THIRD NORN

Loge's host
dances flaming round the rock.
Night's still here.
Let's on with our spinning and song.

SECOND NORN

(to the first)

While we are spinning and singing
the cord has to be stretched.

FIRST NORN

(rises and fastens one end of a golden cord to a branch of the fir tree while she sings)

Though all goes well and ill,
fasten the cord while singing.
At the world ash tree
once I wove,
when, lush and thick,
the stem put forth
with holy and verdurous boughs.
Amid cool shadows
purled a spring.
Whispering wisdom
rippled its waves.
I sang my mystical thoughts.
A valiant god
stepped to drink at the spring,
and he yielded up an eye
as his payment for power.
From the world ash tree
Wotan broke away a branch.

From this wood the hero
shaped the shaft of a spear.
The course of time was long.
Worse grew the wound in the wood.
Leaves fell in their sereness.
Then, blight took the tree.
Sadly the source of the water failed.
All my songs
were measures of woe.
And now no more do I weave beside
    the ash.
So must the fir tree
serve me for fastening the cord.
Sing, O sister—
you take it now—
why was all this so?

SECOND NORN

(winding the cord thrown to her round a projecting rock at the cave's mouth)

Wotan carved on his
mighty spear-shaft
runes stating
truth to pacts must hold.
This haft of the world was his.
A valiant man
destroyed his spear in the strife.
The binding witness
to pacts was shattered to bits.
With that, Wotan
bade his heroes
to hew down the ash
with its boughs,
and to shiver all to splinters.
The ash tree fell.
Evermore dried was the spring.
Therefore the jut
of this rock must hold my cord.
Sing, O sister—
you catch it now—
why is all this so?

THIRD NORN

(catching the cord and casting the end behind her)

The giants' work
yet towers aloft.
There sits Wotan,
and with him
all his assembly,
holy heroes and gods.

1

Gehau'ner Scheite
hohe Schicht,
ragt zu Hauf
rings um die Halle.
Die Welt-Esche war dies einst!
Brennt das Holz
heilig, brünstig und hell,
sengt die Glut
sehrend den glänzenden Saal:
Der ewigen Götter Ende
dämmert ewig da auf.
Wisset ihr noch?
So windet von neuem das Seil;
von Norden wieder
werf' ich's dir nach.
Spinne, Schwester, und singe!
(*Sie hat das Seil der Zweiten, diese es
wieder der Ersten Norn zugeworfen.*)

DIE ERSTE NORN
(*löst das Seil vom Zweige, und knüpft
es während des folgenden Gesanges
wieder an einen andern Ast*)
Dämmert der Tag?
Oder leuchtet die Lohe?
Getrübt trügt sich mein Blick;
nicht hell eracht' ich
das heilig Alte,
da Loge einst
entbrannte in lichter Brunst:
Weisst du, was aus ihm ward?

DIE ZWEITE NORN
(*das zugeworfene Seil wieder um den
Stein windend*)
Durch des Speeres Zauber
zähmte ihn Wotan;
Räte raunt' er dem Gott.
An des Schaftes Runen,
frei sich zu raten,
nagte zehrend sein Zahn.
Da, mit des Speeres
zwingender Spitze
bannte ihn Wotan,
Brünnhilde's Fels zu umbrennen.
Weisst du, was aus ihm wird?

DIE DRITTE NORN
(*das zugeschwungene Seil hinter sich
werfend*)
Des zerschlag'nen Speeres
stechende Splitter
taucht einst Wotan
dem Brünstigen tief in die Brust:
zehrender Brand
zündet da auf;
den wirft der Gott
in der Welt-Esche
zu Hauf geschichtete Scheite.

DIE ZWEITE NORN
Wollt ihr wissen

wann das wird?
Schwinget, Schwestern, das Seil!
(*Sie wirft das Seil der Zweiten, diese
es wieder der Ersten zu.*)

DIE ERSTE NORN
(*das Seil von neuem anknüpfend*)
Die Nacht weicht;
nichts mehr gewahr' ich;
des Seiles Fäden
find' ich nicht mehr;
verflochten ist das Geflecht.
Ein wüstes Gesicht
wirrt mir wütend den Sinn:
Das Rheingold
raubte Alberich einst:
weisst du, was aus ihm ward?

DIE ZWEITE NORN
(*mit mühevoller Hast das Seil um den
Stein windend*)
Des Steines Schärfe
schnitt in das Seil;
nicht fest spannt mehr
der Fäden Gespinnst:
verwirrt ist das Geweb'.
Aus Not und Neid
ragt mir des Niblungen Ring:
Ein rächender Fluch
nagt meiner Fäden Geflecht.
Weisst du, was daraus wird?

DIE DRITTE NORN
(*das zugeworfene Seil hastig fassend*)
Zu locker das Seil,
mir langt es nicht;
soll ich nach Norden
neigen das Ende,
straffer sei es gestreckt!
(*Sie zieht gewaltsam das Seil an, dieses
reisst in der Mitte.*)
Es riss!

DIE ZWEITE
Es riss!

DIE ERSTE
Es riss!

DIE DREI NORNEN
Zu End' ewiges Wissen!
Der Welt melden
Weise nichts mehr.
Hinab zur Mutter, hinab!
(*Sie verschwinden.*)
(*Der Tag, der zuletzt immer heller
gedämmert, bricht vollends an, und
dämpft den Feuerschein in der
Tiefe.*)
(*Siegfried und Brünnhilde treten aus
dem Steingemache auf. Siegfried ist
in vollen Waffen. Brünnhilde führt
ihr Ross beim Zaume.*)

A heap of billets piled up high
forms a pyre
round all the castle.
The world ash tree waits the torch!
When the wood
blazes up to the sky,
when the flame
eats up the glittering hall,
the gods everlasting
will have reached the dusk of their day.
Would you know more?
Then wind up the cord once again.
And catch it now,
it comes from the north
Spin, O sister, while singing.
(*She throws the cord to the second
Norn, who throws it to the first.*)

FIRST NORN
(*unties the cord from the branch and
fastens it to another branch while she
sings.*)
Is that the dawn
or a flickering glimmer?
My woe darkens my gaze.
I scarce remember
the ancient marvels.
When Loge once
broke out into brilliant flame,
tell me, what was his fate?

SECOND NORN
(*again taking the cord, and winding it
round the stone*)
Through the spear's strong magic
Wotan has tamed him.
Loge whispered his lore.
But to gain his freedom,
seizing the spear
he gnawed the runes with his teeth.
Then with the spear-point's
mastering magic,
Wotan made Loge
blaze round the rock of Brünnhilde.
Do you know why this is?

THIRD NORN
(*catching the cord again and casting
it behind her*)
Soon will Wotan,
taking splints of his spear-shaft,
drive them deep
in the breast of the fiery god.
Then with the brand
flaming away,
the god will kindle
the world ash tree
heaped high in billets and faggots.
(*She throws the cord to the second, who
who in turn throws it to the first.*)

SECOND MORN
When will this, though,
come to pass?
Stretch now, sisters, the cord!

FIRST NORN
(*again knotting the cord*)
The night wanes.
Nothing comes further.
I cannot find
the strands of the cord.
The braided work is undone.
A terrible sight
puts my thoughts in a whirl:
the dwarf has robbed
the gold of the Rhine.
Tell me, what was his fate?

SECOND NORN
(*winding the rope round the stone*)
The stone is sharply
cutting the cord.
The spun thread holds
no more as it did:
the web now is awry.
The Nibelung ring
fills me with pain and distress.
A furious curse
gnaws on the strands of my cord.
Tell me what things will come.

THIRD NORN
(*hastily catching the cord thrown to
her*)
The cord is too slack!
It does not stretch!
If I'm to send it northward
it must be stretched
much tighter than that.
(*She pulls on the cord, and it breaks.*)

It breaks!
SECOND NORN
It breaks!
FIRST NORN
It breaks!
ALL THREE
Thus ends wisdom eternal!
The world marks
our wisdom no more.
Away, to Mother, away!
(*They disappear.*)
(*The day, which has been gradually
breaking, now dawns brightly, thus
concealing the distant fire-glow in the
valley.*)
(*Siegfried and Brünnhilde enter from
the cave. Siegfried is in full armor;
Brünnhilde is leading her horse by
the bridle.*)

BRÜNNHILDE

Zu neuen Taten,
teurer Helde,
wie lieb' ich dich,
liess' ich dich nicht?
Ein einzig Sorgen
lässt mich säumen:
dass dir zu wenig
mein Wert gewann!
Was Götter mich wiesen,
gab ich dir,
heiliger Runen
reichen Hort;
doch meiner Stärke
magdlichen Stamm
nahm mir der Held,
dem ich nun mich neige.
Des Wissens bar
doch des Wunsches voll;
an Liebe reich,
doch ledig der Kraft,
mög'st du die Arme
nicht verachten,
die dir nur gönnen,
nicht geben mehr kann.

SIEGFRIED

Mehr gabst du, Wunderfrau,
als ich zu wahren weiss.
Nicht zürne, wenn dein Lehren
mich unbelehret liess!
Ein Wissen doch wahr' ich wohl:
dass mir Brünnhilde lebt;
eine Lehre lernt' ich leicht:
Brünnhilde's zu gedenken!

BRÜNNHILDE

Willst du mir Minne schenken,
gedenke deiner nur,
gedenke deiner Taten!
Gedenk' des wilden Feuers,
das furchtlos du durchschrittest,
da den Fels es rings umbrann!

SIEGFRIED

Brünnhilde zu gewinnen!

BRÜNNHILDE

Gedenk' der beschildeten Frau,
die in tiefem Schlaf du fandest,
der den festen Helm du erbrach'st.

SIEGFRIED

Brünnhilde zu erwecken!

BRÜNNHILDE

Gedenk' der Eide,
die uns einen;

gedenk' der Treue,
die wir tragen;
gedenk' der Liebe,
der wir leben:
Brünnhilde brennt dann ewig
heilig dir in der Brust!
(*Sie umarmt Siegfried.*)

SIEGFRIED

Lass' ich, Liebste, dich hier
in der Lohe heiliger Hut,
zum Tausche deiner Runen
reich' ich dir diesen Ring.
Was der Taten je ich schuf,
dess' Tugend schliesst er ein.
Ich erschlug einen wilden Wurm,
der grimmig lang ihn bewacht.
Nun wahre du seine Kraft
als Weihegruss meiner Treu'!

BRÜNNHILDE

Ihn geiz' ich als einziges Gut!
Für den Ring nun nimm auch mein
  Ross!
Ging sein Lauf mit mir
einst kühn durch die Lüfte,
mit mir
verlor es die mächt'ge Art;
über Wolken hin
auf blitzenden Wettern
nicht mehr
schwingt es sich mutig des Wegs.
Doch wohin du ihn führst
—sei es durch's Feuer—
grauenlos folgt dir Grane;
denn dir, o Helde,
soll er gehorchen!
Du hüt' ihn wohl;
er hört dein Wort:
O, bringe Grane
oft Brünnhilde's Gruss!

SIEGFRIED

Durch deine Tugend allein
soll so ich Taten noch wirken?
Meine Kämpfe kiesest du,
meine Siege kehren zu dir:
Auf deines Rosses Rücken,
in deines Schildes Schirm,
nicht Siegfried acht' ich mich mehr:
Ich bin nur Brünnhilde's Arm!

BRÜNNHILDE

O wäre Brünnhild' deine Seele!

SIEGFRIED

Durch sie entbrennt mir der Mut.

BRÜNNHILDE

So wär'st du Siegfried und Brünnhild'?

BRÜNNHILDE

Unless I left you,
dearest, O hero,
to new exploits,
poor were my love.
A single doubt, though,
still constrains me:
the fear that all
I have given is slight.
I gave you my wisdom
from the gods,
lore from my hoard
of holy runes;
yet you have robbed
the staff of my strength,
my maidenly might.
Now it is gone,
and I live to serve you.
My wisdom's gone,
but my will remains.
I'm rich in love
but lacking in strength.
Do not despise
the wretched woman
who only wishes,
but cannot perform.

SIEGFRIED

More have you given me
than I have wit to know.
So chide not, if your lessons
have left me still untaught.
One thing though I know quite well:
for me Brünnhilde lives.
One thing's not to hard to learn:
Brünnhilde to remember!

BRÜNNHILDE

If you would prove you love me,
recall the goal you had.
Recall your deeds of valor.
recall the magic fire
you stepped through in your daring,
when it blazed around the rock!

SIEGFRIED

Brünnhilde was my purpose!

BRÜNNHILDE

Recall, too, the maid with the shield,
whom you found in magic slumber,
and whose fastened helmet you broke.

SIEGFRIED

Brünnhilde thus was wakened!

BRÜNNHILDE

Recall the pledges
that unite us.

Recall the troths
that we have plighted.
Recall the love
that we have lived by.
Then Brünnhilde's holy flame
will ever burn in your breast!
(*She embraces Siegfried.*)

SIEGFRIED

Now I leave you, my love,
in the blest protection of fire.
For secret runes you taught me
take this ring in exchange.
All the deeds I ever did
obtained their virtue here.
I once conquered a dragon foe
who grimly guarded this ring.
Now keep this powerful charm
as holy pledge of my troth!

BRÜNNHILDE

I'll cherish it more than all else.
For the ring take my stalwart horse.
He could bear me once
with speed through the heavens.
With me
he lost this most mighty art.
He will prance no more
through lightning and thunder,
nor soar
daringly over the clouds.
But wherever you lead—
even through fire—
fearlessly Grane will follow.
For you, O hero,
now are his master!
So hold him well.
he'll heed your word.
Oh, often bring him
fond greetings from me.

SIEGFRIED

Must I achieve all my deeds
only through virtues you give me?
You select my fights for me,
and my victories come from your will.
I stride the steed you gave me,
beneath your sheltering shield—
so now I'm Siegfried no more,
but only Brünnhilde's arm!

BRÜNNHILDE

Oh, were your soul also Brünnhilde's.

SIEGFRIED

Through her alone I have heart.

BRÜNNHILDE

That makes you Siegfried and Brünnhilde.

SIEGFRIED

Wo ich bin bergen sich Beide.

BRÜNNHILDE

So verödet mein Felsensaal?

SIEGFRIED

Vereint fasst er uns zwei!

BRÜNNHILDE

O heilige Götter!
Hehre Geschlechter!
Weidet eu'r Aug'
an dem weihvollen Paar!
Getrennt—wer will es scheiden?
Geschieden—trennt es sich nie!

SIEGFRIED

Heil dir, Brünnhilde,
prangender Stern!

BRÜNNHILDE

Heil dir, Siegfried,
siegendes Licht!

SIEGFRIED

Heil, strahlende Liebe!
Heil, strahlender Stern!
Heil, Brünnhilde! Heil!

BRÜNNHILDE

Heil, strahlendes Leben!
Heil, siegendes Licht!

(*Siegfried leitet das Ross den Felsen
hinab, Brünnhilde blickt ihm vom
Höhensaume lange entzückt nach.
Aus der Tiefe hört man Siegfried's
Horn munter ertönen.—Der Vorhang
fällt.*)

ERSTER AUFZUG

ERSTE SCENE

Die Halle der Gibichungen am Rhein.
*Sie ist dem Hintergrunde zu ganz
offen; diesen nimmt ein freier Uferraum bis zum Flusse hin ein; felsige
Anhöhen umgrenzen das Ufer.*

(*Gunther und Gutrune auf dem Hoch-
sitze, vor dem ein Tisch mit Trink-
gerät steht; Hagen sitzt davor.*)

GUNTHER

Nun hör, Hagen;
sage mir, Held:
sitz' ich herrlich am Rhein,
Gunther zu Gibich's Ruhm?

HAGEN

Dich echt genannten
acht' ich zu neiden;
die beid' uns Brüder gebar,
Frau Grimhild' liess mich's begreifen.

GUNTHER

Dich neide ich;
nicht neide mich du!
Erbt ich Erstlingsart,
Weisheit ward dir allein:
Halbbrüderzwist
bezwang sich nie besser;
deinem Rat nur red' ich Lob,
frag' ich dich nach meinem Ruhm.

HAGEN

So schelt' ich den Rat,
da schlecht noch dein Ruhm;
denn hohe Güter weiss ich,
die der Gibichung noch nicht gewann.

GUNTHER

Verschwieg'st du sie,
so schelte auch ich.

HAGEN

In sommerlich reifer Stärke
seh' ich Gibich's Stamm,
dich, Gunther, unbeweibt,
dich, Gutrun', ohne Mann.

GUNTHER

Wen rät'st du nun zu frei'n,
dass unsrem Ruhm es fromm'?

HAGEN

Ein Weib weiss ich,
das herrlichste der Welt:
Auf Felsen hoch ihr Sitz;
ein Feuer umbrennt ihren Saal:
nur wer durch das Feuer bricht,
darf Brünnhilde's Freier sein.

GUNTHER

Vermag das mein Mut zu besteh'n?

HAGEN

Einem Stärk'ren noch, ist's nur
bestimmt.

GUNTHER

Wer ist der streitlichste Mann?

HAGEN

Siegfried, der Wälsungen Spross,
der ist der stärkste Held.
Ein Zwillingspaar,
von Liebe bezwungen,
Siegmund und Sieglinde
zeugten den echtesten Sohn.
Der im Walde mächtig erwuchs,
den wünsch' ich Gutrun' zum Mann.

SIEGFRIED
Where I am, both of us harbor.

BRÜNNHILDE
Is my rock-hall deserted then?

SIEGFRIED
It makes two into one.

BRÜNNHILDE
O holy immortals,
noble protectors!
Joy in the sight
of a love such as ours.
Apart—none can divide us.
Divided—never apart.

SIEGFRIED
Hail, O Brünnhilde,
radiant star!

BRÜNNHILDE
Hail, O Siegfried,
conquering light!

SIEGFRIED
Hail, love full of glory!
Hail, radiant star!
Hail, Brünnhilde, hail!

BRÜNNHILDE
Hail, love full of glory!
Hail, conquering light!

(*Siegfried quickly leads the horse to the
rocky descent, while Brünnhilde gazes
after him from the height for a long
while. From the valley the merry
sound of Siegfried's horn is heard.
The curtain falls.*)

ACT ONE

FIRST SCENE

The Hall of the Gibichungs
on the Rhine

*The back is quite open, showing a flat
shore down to the river; rocky heights
around. Gunther and Gutrune are on
a throne, before which is a table with
drinking vessels. Hagen is seated before it.*

GUNTHER
Now hark, Hagen,
tell me the truth:
is my throne by the Rhine
helpful to Gibich's fame?

HAGEN
To know your glory
rouses my envy,
but she, your mother and mine,
Dame Grimhild, gave me to know this.

GUNTHER
I envy you,
you envy me not!
Though I'm lord and heir,
wisdom is yours alone.
How better end
the strife of half-brothers!
Just to ask you of my fame
is to give your judgment praise.

HAGEN
The blame must be mine
your fame is not great:
I know of high advantage
that the Gibichung has not yet won.

GUNTHER
I'll blame you too
unless I'm told.

HAGEN
The Gibichung race has reached
its ripe and summer bloom:
you, Gunther, still unwed,
you, Gutrune, still no mate.

GUNTHER
Whom would you have me woo
that we may build our fame?

HAGEN
A rare woman,
none nobler in the world.
Her seat's a rocky height,
a fire flames round her abode.
The one who breaks through that fire
finds Brünnhilde, a maid to woo.

GUNTHER
And have I the courage for that?

HAGEN
It is meant to be for one more strong.

GUNTHER
Who is this valorous man?

HAGEN
Siegfried, the Volsungen son;
he is the mighty man.
A twin-born pair,
in loving attraction,
Siegmund and Sieglinde,
begot a legitimate son,
who has grown to strength in the
    woods—
this hero Gutrune should wed.

GUTRUNE
Welche Tat schuf er so tapfer,
dass als herrlichster Held er genannt?

HAGEN
Vor Neidhöhle
den Niblungenhort
bewachte ein riesiger Wurm:
Siegfried schloss ihm
den freislichen Schlund,
erschlug ihn mit siegendem Schwert.
Solch' ungeheurer Tat
enttagte des Helden Ruhm.

GUNTHER
Vom Niblungenhort vernahm ich,
er birgt den neidlichsten Schatz?

HAGEN
Wer wohl ihn zu nützen wüsst',
dem neigte sich wahrlich die Welt.

GUNTHER
Und Siegfried hat ihn erkämpft?

HAGEN
Knecht sind die Niblungen ihm.

GUNTHER
Und Brünnhild' gewänne nur er?

HAGEN
Keinem and'ren wiche die Brunst.

GUNTHER
(unwillig sich vom Sitze erhebend)
Was weckst du Zweifel und Zwist?
Was ich nicht zwingen soll,
danach zu verlangen
machst du mir Lust?

HAGEN
Brächte Siegfried
die Braut dir heim,
wär' dann nicht Brünnhilde dein?

GUNTHER
Was zwänge den frohen Mann
für mich die Braut zu frei'n?

HAGEN
Ihn zwänge bald deine Bitte,
bänd' ihn Gutrun zuvor.

GUTRUNE
Du Spötter, böser Hagen!
Wie sollt' ich Siegfried binden?
Ist er der herrlichste
Held der Welt,
der Erde holdeste Frauen
friedeten längst ihn schon.

HAGEN
(sich vertraulich zu Gutrune hinnei-
gend)
Gedenk' des Trankes im Schrein;
vertrau' mir, der ihn gewann.
Den Helden, dess' du verlangst,
bindet er liebend an dich.
Träte nun Siegfried ein,
genöss' er des würzigen Trank's,
dass vor dir ein Weib er ersah,
dass je ein Weib ihm genaht'—
vergessen müsst' er dess' ganz.
Nun redet:
Wie dünkt euch Hagen's Rat?

GUNTHER
(der wieder an den Tisch getreten und,
auf ihn gelehnt, aufmerksam zuge-
hört hat)
Gepriesen sei Grimhild',
die uns den Bruder gab!

GUTRUNE
Möcht' ich Siegfried je erseh'n!

GUNTHER
Wie fänden ihn wir auf?
(Aus dem Hintergrund vernimmt
man ein Horn.)

HAGEN
Jagt er auf Taten
wonnig umher,
zum engen Tann
wird ihm die Welt:
wohl stürmt er in rastloser Jagd
auch zu Gibich's Strand an den Rhein.

GUNTHER
Willkommen hiess' ich ihn gern.
(Siegfried's Horn lässt sich von Ferne
vernehmen. Sie lauschen.)
Vom Rhein her tönt das Horn.

HAGEN
(ist an das Ufer gegangen, späht den
Fluss hinab und ruft zurück)
In einem Nachen Held und Ross!
Der bläst so munter das Horn!
Ein gemächlicher Schlag,
wie von müss'ger Hand,
treibt jach den Kahn
wider den Strom;
so rüstiger Kraft
in des Ruder's Schwung
rühmt sich nur der,
der den Wurm erschlug.
Siegfried ist es, sicher kein And'rer!

GUNTHER
Jagt er vorbei?

GUTRUNE

Tell me deeds done by this Siegfried,
that he merits a hero's renown.

HAGEN

At hate cavern
the Nibelung hoard
was watched by a dragon foe.
Siegfried closed up
his terrible maw,
destroyed him with conquering sword.
Such an unheard-of deed
gave wings to the hero's fame.

GUNTHER

The Nibelung hoard, they tell me,
includes some wonderful wealth.

HAGEN

The one who best knows its use
will bend all the world to his will.

GUNTHER

And Siegfried won it in war?

HAGEN

Now are the Nibelungs his slaves.

GUNTHER

Can Brünnhilde be won by none else?

HAGEN

No one else can stifle the blaze.

GUNTHER

(rising in displeasure)

Why waken discord and doubt?
Why do you stir my mind
to long for a treasure
I cannot win?

HAGEN

But if Siegfried
should fetch the bride,
would not Brünnhilde be yours?

GUNTHER

What power could get this man
to woo the bride for me?

HAGEN

If Gutrune worked an enchantment
Siegfried then would be bound.

GUTRUNE

You mocker, wicked Hagen!
How can I work enchantment?
If he's the greatest
of men on earth,
the fairest women on earth
must surely have had his love.

HAGEN

(confidentially to Gutrune)

Recall the drink in the chest,
and trust in me who won the charm.
The hero for whom you long
soon can be bound to your love.
Siegfried need only come
and taste of the magical drink.
That he'd seen a woman ere you,
or that one ever came near,
would wholly pass from his mind.
Now tell me,
how like you Hagen's plan?

GUNTHER

(has again approached the table and
listened attentively, leaning on it)

All praise be to Grimhild,
for brother wise as this!

GUTRUNE

I would love to meet this man.

GUNTHER

But how can he be found?

(A horn is heard in the distance.)

HAGEN

When he is gaily
questing for fame,
the world becomes
a narrow woods.
Be sure in his quests he will reach
even Gibich's strand on the Rhine.

GUNTHER

Surely I'll welcome him well!

(Siegfried's horn is again heard in the
distance, but nearer. They listen.)

The sound comes from the Rhine.

HAGEN

(goes to the bank, looks up and down
the river)

Within a boat a horse and man.
He blows a rollicking horn!
With a casual stroke,
as from idle hand,
he drives the boat
speedily on.
So practised a hand
when he swings the scull
comes but from him
who has done that deed.
Siegfried it is, surely no other!

GUNTHER

Will he pass by?

HAGEN
*(durch die hohlen Hände nach dem
Flusse zu rufend)*
Hoiho! Wohin,
du heit'rer Held?

SIEGFRIED'S STIMME
(aus der Ferne, vom Flusse her)
Zu Gibich's starkem Sohne.

HAGEN
Zu seiner Halle entbiet' ich dich.
(Siegfried erscheint im Kahn am Ufer.)
Hieher! Hier lege an!
Heil Siegfried! Teurer Held!
(Siegfried legt an.)
*(Gunther ist zu Hagen an das Ufer
getreten. Hagen schliesst den Kahn
mit der Kette am Ufer fest. Siegfried
springt mit dem Ross an den Strand.)*
SIEGFRIED
Wer ist Gibich's Sohn?
*(Siegfried an sein Ross gelehnt bleibt
ruhig am Kahne stehen. Gutrune
blickt vom Hochsitz aus in staunen-
der Bewunderung auf ihn. Gunther
will freundlichen Gruss bieten. Alle
sind in gegenseitiger stummer Betrachtung gefesselt.)*
GUNTHER
Gunther, ich, den du suchst.

SIEGFRIED
Dich hört' ich rühmen
weit am Rhein:
nun ficht mit mir,
oder sei mein Freund!

GUNTHER
Lass' den Kampf!
Sei willkommen!

SIEGFRIED
Wo berg' ich mein Ross?

HAGEN
Ich biet' ihm Rast.

SIEGFRIED
Du rief'st mich Siegfried:
sah'st du mich schon?

HAGEN
Ich kannte dich nur
an deiner Kraft.

SIEGFRIED
Wohl hüte mir Grane!
Du hieltest nie
von edlerer Zucht
am Zaume ein Ross.
*(Hagen führt das Ross rechts hinter die
Halle ab, und kehrt bald darauf
wieder zurück. Gunther schreitet mit
Siegfried in die Halle vor.)*

GUNTHER
Begrüsse froh, o Held,
die Halle meines Vaters;
wohin du schreitest,
was du ersiehst,
das achte nun dein Eigen:
Dein ist mein Erbe,
Land und Leute:
Hilf mein Leib meinem Eide!
Mich selbst geb' ich zum Mann.

SIEGFRIED
Nicht Land noch Leute biete ich,
noch Vaters Haus und Hof:
einzig erbt' ich
den eig'nen Leib;
lebend zehr' ich den auf.
Nur ein Schwert hab' ich,
selbst geschmiedet:
Hilf mein Schwert meinem Eide!
Das biet' ich mit mir zum Bund.

HAGEN
Doch des Niblungenhortes
nennt die Märe dich Herrn?

SIEGFRIED
Des Schatzes vergass ich fast;
so schätz' ich sein müss'ges Gut!
In einer Höhle liess' ich's liegen,
wo ein Wurm es einst bewacht.

HAGEN
Und nichts entnahm'st du ihm?

SIEGFRIED
*(auf das stählerne Netzgewirk deutend,
das er im Gürtel hängen hat)*
Dies Gewirk, unkund seiner Kraft.

HAGEN
Den Tarnhelm kenn' ich,
der Niblungen künstliches Werk;
er taugt, bedeckt er dein Haupt,
dir zu tauschen jede Gestalt.
Verlangt dich's an fernsten Ort,
er entführt flugs dich dahin.
Sonst nichts entnahm'st du dem Hort?

SIEGFRIED
Einen Ring.

HAGEN
Den hütest du wohl?

SIEGFRIED
Den hütet ein hehres Weib.

HAGEN
(für sich)
Brünnhild' . . .

HAGEN
(*making a trumpet of his hands and
shouting*)
Hoiho! Where to,
you merry man?

SIEGFRIED'S VOICE
(*from the distance, on the river*)
To Gibich's mighty offspring.

HAGEN
I bid you welcome to Gibich's hall!
(*Siegfried's boat appears.*)
This way! Here come ashore!
Hail Siegfried! Valiant man!
(*Gunther comes down and joins Hagen.
Siegfried brings his boat to the shore.
Hagen makes it fast with the chain.
Siegfried springs ashore with his
horse.*)

SIEGFRIED
Who is Gibich's son?
(*He leans on his horse, remaining quietly standing by the boat. Gutrune
gazes at him from her throne in
astonishment. Gunther prepares to
offer him friendly greetings. All stand
fixed in silent mutual contemplation.*)

GUNTHER
Gunther, I, whom you seek.

SIEGFRIED
Your fame is wide
all round the Rhine.
Now fight with me
or else be my friend!

GUNTHER
Speak of peace:
you are welcome!

SIEGFRIED
A place for my horse?

HAGEN
I'll see to that.

SIEGFRIED
You called me Siegfried.
When did we meet?

HAGEN
I knew who you were
just by your strength.

SIEGFRIED
Take care of my Grane!
You've never held
a horse by the bit
so noble in breed.
(*Hagen leads the horse away, and returns immediately. Gunther advances
into the hall with Siegfried.*)

GUNTHER
Well, hero, hail with joy
the homestead of my father.
The ground you tread on,
all things you see,
treat as your own from henceforth.
Yours is my birthright,
land and people—
add my limbs to this promise,
myself—all these are yours.

SIEGFRIED
I offer neither men nor land,
nor father's house and court.
All I own
is my life and limbs;
these I spend as I live.
Just a sword is there,
which I welded.
So I swear by my weapon.
My sword and myself are yours.

HAGEN
Yet from tales that are told
you won the Nibelung hoard.

SIEGFRIED
I nearly forgot that store.
What good is an idle wealth?
I let it stay there in its cavern,
where a dragon once kept guard.

HAGEN
You took no part of it?

SIEGFRIED
(*pointing to the steel network that
hangs in his girdle*)
Just this piece, which I cannot use.

HAGEN
The Tarnhelm, truly,
the Nibelungs' wonderful work!
It serves, when set on your head,
to transform you to any shape.
And if you would travel far,
it transports you in a trice.
And was that all that you took?

SIEGFRIED
Just a ring.

HAGEN
You're keeping it well?

SIEGFRIED
A wonderful woman is.

HAGEN
(*aside*)
Brünnhilde!

GUNTHER

Nicht, Siegfried, sollst du mir tauschen,
Tand gäb' ich für das Geschmeid,
nähmst all' mein Gut du dafür!
Ohn' Entgelt dien' ich dir gern.
(*Hagen ist zu Gutrune's Türe gegang-
en und öffnet sie jetzt. Gutrune tritt
heraus: sie trägt ein gefülltes Trinkhorn und naht damit Siegfried.*)

GUTRUNE

Willkommen Gast,
in Gibich's Haus!
Seine Tochter reicht dir den Trank.

SIEGFRIED

(*neigt sich ihr freundlich und ergreift
das Horn; er hält es gedankenvoll vor
sich hin, und sagt leise*)
Vergäss' ich Alles,
was du mir gab'st,
von einer Lehre
lass' ich doch nie:
Den ersten Trunk
zu treuer Minne,
Brünnhilde, bring' ich dir!
(*Er trinkt und reicht das Horn Gutrune zurück, welche, verschämt und
verwirrt, ihre Augen vor ihm nieder-
schlägt.*)

SIEGFRIED

(*mit schnell entbrannter Leidenschaft
den Blick auf sie heftend*)
Die so mit dem Blitz
den Blick du mir sengst,
was senkst du dein Auge vor mir?
(*Gutrune schlägt, errötend, das Auge
zu ihm auf.*)
Ha schönstes Weib!
Schliesse den Blick!
Das Herz in der Brust
brennt mir sein Strahl:
zu feurigen Strömen fühl' ich
ihn zehrend zünden mein Blut!
(*mit bebender Stimme*)
Gunther—wie heisst deine Schwester?

GUNTHER

Gutrune.

SIEGFRIED

Sind's gute Runen,
die ihrem Aug' ich entrate?
(*Er fasst Gutrune mit feurigem Un-
gestüm bei der Hand.*)
Deinem Bruder bot ich mich zum
Mann;
der Stolze schlug mich aus:
Trüg'st du, wie er, mir Uebermut,
böt' ich mich dir zum Bund?
(*Gutrune neigt demütig das Haupt,
und mit einer Gebärde, als fühle sie
sich seiner nicht wert, verlässt sie*

*wankenden Schrittes wieder die
Halle.*)

SIEGFRIED

(*blickt ihr, wie festgezaubert, nach,
von Hagen und Gunther aufmerksam
beobachtet; dann, ohne sich umzu-
wenden, fragt er:*)
Hast du, Gunther, ein Weib?

GUNTHER

Nicht freit' ich noch,
und einer Frau
soll' ich mich schwerlich freu'n!
Auf eine setzt' ich den Sinn,
die kein Rat mir je gewinnt.

SIEGFRIED

Was wär' dir versagt,
steh' ich zu dir?

GUNTHER

Auf Felsen hoch ihr Sitz;
ein Feuer umbrennt den Saal.

SIEGFRIED

(*verwundert, und wie um eines längst
Vergessenen sich zu entsinnen, wie-
derholt leise*):
"Auf Felsen hoch ihr Sitz?
ein Feuer umbrennt den Saal . . .?"

GUNTHER

Nur wer durch das Feuer bricht—

SIEGFRIED

"Nur wer durch das Feuer bricht"?

GUNTHER

—darf Brünnhilde's Freier sein.
Nun darf ich den Fels nicht erklimmen;
das Feuer verglimmt mir nie!

SIEGFRIED
(*heftig auffahrend*)
Ich fürchte kein Feuer;
für dich frei ich die Frau.
Denn dein Mann bin ich,
und mein Mut ist dein—
gewinn' ich mir Gutrun' zum Weib.

GUNTHER

Gutrune gönn' ich dir gerne.

SIEGFRIED

Brünnhilde bring' ich dir.

GUNTHER

Wie willst du sie täuschen?

SIEGFRIED

Durch des Tarnhelm's Trug
tausch' ich mir deine Gestalt.

GUNTHER

So stelle Eide zum Schwur!

GUNTHER

I've nothing but toys to give,
even by adding my all.
I will serve you freely, with joy.
(*Hagen has gone to Gutrune's door
and now opens it. Gutrune enters and
approaches Siegfried with a drinking
horn.*)

GUTRUNE

Welcome, O guest,
to Gibich's house!
It's his daughter gives you the drink.

SIEGFRIED

(*bows pleasantly and takes the horn; he
holds it thoughtfully before him, and
says softly:*)
Were all forgot
of what you had given,
one lesson
would stay in my mind.
This first of drinks
to love that's faithful,
Brünnhilde, is to you!
(*He drinks, and hands back the horn
to Gutrune, who, ashamed and con-
fused, casts down her eyes.*)

SIEGFRIED

(*gazing at her with sudden passion*)
You beautiful one,
whose looks fire my heart,
why cast down your eyes before mine?
       (*Gutrune looks up, blushing.*)
Ha, fairest maid!
Hide that bright gaze.
The heart in my breast
burns from its beams.
Their fiery force consumes
all the blood that flows in my veins!
          (*with trembling voice*)
Gunther—what name has your sister?

GUNTHER

Gutrune.

SIEGFRIED

But are they runes of good
that I read in her glances?
(*He ardently seizes Gutrune's hand.*)
When I sought to be your brother's
   man,
the haughty one refused.
Would you be just as arrogant
if I asked you the same?
(*Gutrune humbly droops her head and
then, with deprecating gesture, leaves
the hall again with trembling steps.*)

SIEGFRIED

(*closely observed by Hagen and Gun-
ther, gazes after her as if spellbound.
Then, without turning, he asks:*)
Have you, Gunther, a wife?

GUNTHER

I'm not yet wed,
nor, do I think,
likely to find a wife!
My mind is set though on one,
but advice will not avail.

SIEGFRIED

But how could you fail
were I to help?

GUNTHER

She dwells upon a rock;
a fire surrounds her home.

SIEGFRIED

(*repeating the words, as if trying to
remember something half-forgotten*)
"She dwells upon a rock;
a fire surrounds her home . . . ?"

GUNTHER

But he who can brave that fire—

SIEGFRIED

"But he who can brave that fire . . . ?"

GUNTHER

wins Brünnhilde for his wife.
I dare not attempt the ascension;
the fire won't fade for me.

SIEGFRIED

(*with a sudden start*)
I—fear not the fire:
the bride soon shall be yours.
I'm your man, henceforth,
and my strength is yours—
provided that Gutrune is mine.

GUNTHER

Gladly I'll grant you my sister.

SIEGFRIED

Soon you'll see Brünnhilde here.

GUNTHER

But how will you fool her?

SIEGFRIED

Through the Tarnhelm's magic,
which will give me your form.

GUNTHER

So then an oath must be sworn!

SIEGFRIED

Blutbrüderschaft
schwöre ein Eid!

(*Hagen füllt ein Trinkhorn mit fri-*
schem Wein; Siegfried und Gunther
ritzen sich mit ihren Schwertern die
Arme, und halten diese einen Augen-
blick über das Trinkhorn.)

SIEGFRIED UND GUNTHER

Blühenden Lebens
labendes Blut
träufelt' ich in den Trank.
Bruderbrünstig
mutig gemischt,
blüh' im Trank unser Blut!
Treue trink' ich dem Freund!
Froh und frei
entblühe dem Bund
Blutbrüderschaft heut'!
Bricht ein Bruder den Bund,
trügt den Treuen der Freund,
was in Tropfen heut'
hold wir tranken,
in Strahlen ström' es dahin,
fromme Sühne dem Freund!
So biet' ich den Bund!
So trink' ich dir Treu'!

(*Sie trinken nach einander, jeder zur*
Hälfte; dann zerschlägt Hagen, der
während des Schwures zur Seite ge-
standen, mit seinem Schwerte das
Horn. Siegfried und Gunther reichen
sich die Hände.)

SIEGFRIED

(*zu Hagen*)

Was nahmst du am Eide nicht teil?

HAGEN

Mein Blut verdürb' euch den Trank!
Nicht fliesst mir's echt
und edel wie euch;
störrisch und kalt
stockt's in mir;
nicht will's die Wange mir röten.
Drum bleib' ich fern
vom feurigen Bund.

GUNTHER

(*zu Siegfried*)

Lass' den unfrohen Mann!

SIEGFRIED

Frisch auf die Fahrt!
Dort liegt mein Schiff;

schnell führt es zum Felsen.
Eine Nacht am Ufer
harr'st du im Nachen;
die Frau fährst du dann heim.
(*Er geht zum Ufer.*)

GUNTHER

Rastest du nicht zuvor?

SIEGFRIED

Um die Rückkehr ist's mir jach.
(*Er winkt Gunther.*)

GUNTHER

Du Hagen! Bewache die Halle!
(*Er folgt Siegfried zum Ufer. Während*
Gunther und Siegfried, nachdem sie
ihre Waffen darin niedergelegt, im
Schiff das Segel aufstecken und alles
zur Abfahrt bereit machen, nimmt
Hagen sein Speer und Schild. Gu-
trune erscheint an der Tür ihres
Gemaches, gerade als Siegfried das
Schiff abstösst.)

GUTRUNE

Wohin eilen die Schnellen?

HAGEN

(*während er sich gemächlich mit Schild*
und Speer vor der Halle nieder-
setzt)
Zu Schiff, Brünnhild' zu frei'n.

GUTRUNE

Siegfried?

HAGEN

Sieh', wie's ihn treibt,
zum Weib dich zu gewinnen!
(*Siegfried und Gunther fahren ab.*)

GUTRUNE

Siegfried—mein!
(*Sie geht, lebhaft erregt, in ihr Gemach*
zurück.)

HAGEN

Hier sitz' ich zur Wacht,
wahre den Hof,
wehre die Halle dem Feind.
Gibich's Sohne
wehet der Wind;
auf Werben fährt er dahin.
Ihm führt das Steuer
ein starker Held,
Gefahr ihm will er besteh'n:
Die eig'ne Braut
ihm bringt er zum Rhein;
mir aber bringt er den Ring!
Ihr freien Söhne,
frohe Gesellen,
segelt nur lustig dahin!
Dünkt er euch niedrig,
ihr dient ihm doch—
des Niblungen Sohn

SIEGFRIED

Blood-brotherhood
hallowed by oath!

(*Hagen fills a drinking horn with wine;
he holds it out to Siegfried and Gunther, who cut their arms with their
swords and hold them over the horn
for a moment; they then each lay
two fingers on the horn, which Hagen
continues to hold between them.*)

SIEGFRIED, GUNTHER

Vigorous blood
of flowering life
drops straight into the drink.
Brothers' courage
blends in our oath.
See the glow of our blood.
Troth I drink to my friend!
Glad and free
upspring from our league
blood-brotherhood now!
But if brother in blood
breaks his vow to his friend,
what we two today
hereby are drinking
will gush most bitterly forth,
till requital be made.
So—here's to our league!

So—here's to good faith!

(*Gunther drinks and hands the horn to
Siegfried, who finishes the draught
and holds the empty horn to Hagen.
Hagen breaks the horn in two with
his sword. Gunther and Siegfried
clasp hands.*)

SIEGFRIED

(*to Hagen*)

Why did you not join in the oath?

HAGEN

My blood would ruin the drink.
It flows not clear and noble like yours;
sluggish and cold,
scarcely stirs.
My cheeks can hardly be reddened.
It's not for me,
this hot-headed league!

GUNTHER

(*to Siegfried*)

Pay no heed to this churl.

SIEGFRIED

Fresh for the trip,
there lies my skiff.

Quick, on to the mountain.
Wait on shore for one night,
till I arrive there,
and then bear home the bride.

(*He starts for the shore.*)

GUNTHER

Will you not first take rest?

SIEGFRIED

My return trip will be fast.

(*He beckons Gunther.*)

GUNTHER

You, Hagen, take care of the homestead!

(*He follows Siegfried. While Siegfried
and Gunther, after putting their
swords in the boat, hoist the sail and
make ready for departure, Hagen
takes up his spear and shield. Gutrune appears at the door of her
chamber just as Siegfried pushes out
the boat to the middle of the stream.*)

GUTRUNE

And now, where are they speeding?

HAGEN

(*seating himself comfortably before the
hall with spear and shield*)

To court Brünnhilde for bride.

GUTRUNE

Siegfried?

HAGEN

See how he strives
for you, wanting to win you!

(*Siegfried and Gunther fare away.*)

GUTRUNE

Siegfried—mine?

(*She goes back to her chamber in much
emotion.*)

HAGEN

I sit here and wait,
keeping the house,
guarding the place against foes.
Gibich's son
is blown by the wind,
as off a-wooing he goes.
A mighty hero
is at the helm,
to brave what danger may come.
And down the Rhine
he'll bring his own bride.
But he will bring me—the ring!
You hearty brothers,
merry companions,
sail on your rollicking way!
Though he seems abject,
you yet shall serve
the Nibelung's son.

ZWEITE SCENE
Die Felsenhöhe.
(wie im Vorspiel)
BRÜNNHILDE
(*sitzt am Eingange des Steingemaches
und betrachtet in stummem Sinnen
Siegfried's Ring: von wonniger Erinnerung überwältigt, bedeckt sie ihn
dann mit Küssen—als sie plötzlich
ein fernes Geräusch vernimmt; sie
lauscht, und späht zur Seite in den
Hintergrund. Dann wendet sie sich
wieder zu dem Ring.—Ein feuriger
Blitz.—Brünnhilde lauscht von neuem und späht nach der Ferne, von
woher eine finstere Gewitterwolke
dem Felsensaume zuzieht.*)
Altgewohntes Geräusch
raunt meinem Ohr die Ferne.
Ein Luftross jagt
im Laufe daher;
auf der Wolke fährt es
wetternd zum Fels!
Wer fand mich Einsame auf?

WALTRAUTE'S STIMME
(*aus der Ferne*)
Brünnhilde! Schwester!
Schläfst oder wachst du?

BRÜNNHILDE
(*fährt vom Sitze auf*)
Waltraute's Ruf,
so wonnig mir kund!
Kommst du, Schwester,
schwing'st dich kühn zu mir her?
(*in die Szene rufend*)
Dort im Tann
—dir noch vertraut—
steige vom Ross
und stell' den Renner zur Rast.
(*Sie stürmt in den Tann, von wo ein
starkes Geräusch, gleich einem Gewit-
terschlage, sich vernehmen lässt. Sie
kommt in heftiger Bewegung mit
Waltraute zurück; sie bleibt freudig
erregt, ohne Waltraute's ängstliche
Scheu zu beachten.*)
Komm'st du zu mir?
Bist du so kühn?
Mag'st ohne Grauen
Brünnhild' bieten den Gruss?

WALTRAUTE
Einzig dir nur
galt meine Eile.

BRÜNNHILDE
So wagtest du, Brünnhild' zulieb,
Walvater's Bann zu brechen?
Oder wie? o sag'!

wär' wider mich
Wotan's Sinn erweicht?
Als dem Gott entgegen
Siegmund ich schützte,
fehlend—ich weiss es—
erfüllt' ich doch seinen Wunsch.
Dass sein Zorn sich verzogen,
weiss ich auch;
denn verschloss er mich gleich in Schlaf,
fesselt' er mich auf den Fels,
wies er dem Mann mich zur Magd,
der am Weg mich fänd' und erweckt
meiner bangen Bitte
doch gab er Gunst:
mit zehrendem Feuer
umzog er den Fels,
dem Zagen zu wehren den Weg.
So zur Seligsten
schuf mich die Strafe:
Der herrlichste Held
gewann mich zum Weib!
In seiner Liebe
leucht' und lach' ich heut' auf.
(*Sie umarmt Waltraute unter stürmi-
schen Freudenbezeigungen.*)
Lockte dich Schwester mein Los?
An meiner Wonne
willst du dich weiden,
teilen, was mich betraf?

WALTRAUTE
Teilen den Taumel,
der dich Törin erfasst?
Ein and'res bewog mich in Angst
zu brechen Wotan's Gebot.

BRÜNNHILDE
Angst und Furcht
fesseln dich Arme?
So verzieh der Strenge noch nicht?
Du zagst vor des Strafenden Zorn?

WALTRAUTE
Dürft' ich ihn fürchten,
meiner Angst fänd' ich ein End!

BRÜNNHILDE
Staunend versteh' ich dich nicht.

WALTRAUTE
Wehre der Wallung:
achtsam höre mich an!
Nach Walhall wieder
drängt mich die Angst,
die von Walhall hierher mich trieb.

BRÜNNHILDE
Was ist's mit den ewigen Göttern?

SECOND SCENE

The Valkyries' Rock

Brünnhilde is sitting at the mouth of the cave in silent thought. Moved by blissful memories, she covers the ring with kisses. Distant thunder is heard; she looks up and listens. She turns to the ring again. A flash of lightning. Again she listens, and looks into the distance, whence a dark thunder-cloud is moving toward the rock.

BRÜNNHILDE

Once-familiar sounds
near like a rushing tempest.
A horse comes flying
through the air.
He is riding through
the clouds to this rock.
Who seeks the lonely one here?

WALTRAUTE'S VOICE

(from the distance)

Brünnhilde! Sister!
Wake to my tidings!
(Brünnhilde starts up.)

BRÜNNHILDE

Waltraute's cry,
so welcome to hear!
Valiant sister,
have you dared to fly here?
(calling)
See the pines.
As oft of old,
get off your steed:
allow the runner a rest.

(She rushes into the pine woods, from whence is heard a mighty sound as of a thunderbolt. She returns, profoundly moved, with Waltraute. She appears happy, not noticing Waltraute's anguished countenance.)

So you have come?
Are you that bold,
daring to seek me,
Brünnhilde, banished from home!

WALTRAUTE

I have come in haste
for your sake.

BRÜNNHILDE

Was love for me
cause why you broke
Valfather's stern commandment?

Or what else? O say!
Has Wotan's heart
softened at my plight?
When I sheltered Siegmund,
braving our father,
wrongly—I know it—
I yet fulfilled his desire.
And I knew that his anger
was no more.
For though sealing my eyes in sleep,
binding me fast to this rock,
giving me up to the man
who should find me here and awake me,
yet he heard my prayer,
and quelled my fear,
surrounding my rock
with a terrible fire,
to frighten all cowards away.
So my punishment
turned to a blessing:
the noblest of heroes
won me for wife!
Blest in his love
I bask in light and delight.
(She embraces Waltraute joyfully.)
Were you allured by my fate?
Do you desire
to share in my pleasures,
feast on these joys of mine?

WALTRAUTE

Share in the tumult
which you foolishly chose?
Another thing drove me in fear
to brave the will of the god.

BRÜNNHILDE

Fear and dread
hold you in terror.
So his wrath has never let up.
You fear his full punishment's force.

WALTRAUTE

If I could fear him
then my grief soon would be gone.

BRÜNNHILDE

Really, I don't understand.

WALTRAUTE

Master your emotion:
heed the words I must say.
My terror drives me
back to Valhall,
which from Valhall drove me to you.

BRÜNNHILDE

What's wrong with the gods of the
heavens?

WALTRAUTE

Höre mit Sinn was ich dir sage!
Seit er von dir geschieden,
zur Schlacht nicht mehr
schickte uns Wotan;
irr und ratlos
ritten wir ängstlich zu Heer.
Walhall's mutige Helden
mied Walvater:
einsam zu Ross
ohne Ruh' und Rast
durchschweift er als Wandrer die Welt.
Jüngst kehrte er heim:
in der Hand hielt er
seines Speeres Splitter;
die hatte ein Held ihm geschlagen.
Mit stummem Wink
Walhall's Edle
wies er zum Forst,
die Welt-Esche zu fällen;
des Stammes Scheite
hiess er sie schichten
zu ragendem Hauf
rings um der Seligen Saal.
Der Götter Rat
liess er berufen;
den Hochsitz nahm
heilig er ein;
Ihm zu Seiten
hiess er die Bangen sich setzen,
in Ring und Reih'
die Hall' erfüllen die Helden.
So sitzt er,
sagt kein Wort,
auf hehrem Sitze
stumm und ernst,
des Speers Splitter
fest in der Faust;
Holda's Aepfel
rührt er nicht an.
Staunen und Bangen
binden starr die Götter.
Seiner Raben beide
sandt' er auf Reise;
kehrten die einst
mit guter Kunde zurück,
dann noch einmal
—zum letzten Mal—
lächelte ewig der Gott.
Seine Knie' umwindend
liegen wir Walküren:
blind bleibt er
den flehenden Blicken;
uns alle verzehrt
Zagen und endlose Angst.
An seine Brust
presst' ich mich weinend:

da brach sich sein Blick—
er gedachte, Brünnhilde, dein'!
Tief seufzte er auf,
schloss das Auge,
und wie im Traume
raunt' er das Wort;
"Des tiefen Rheines Töchtern
gäbe den Ring sie wieder zurück
von des Fluches Last
erlöst wär' Gott und Welt!"
Da sann ich nach:
von seiner Seite
durch stumme Reihen
stahl ich mich fort;
in heimlicher Hast
bestieg ich mein Ross
und ritt im Sturme zu dir.
Dich, o Schwester,
beschwör' ich nun:
Was du vermagst,
vollend' es dein Mut!
Ende der Ewigen Qual!

(Sie hat sich vor Brünnhilde niederge-
    worfen.)

BRÜNNHILDE

Welch' banger Träume Mären
meldest du Traurige mir!
Der Götter heiligem
Himmelsnebel
bin ich Törin enttaucht:
nicht fass' ich, was ich erfahre.
Wirr und wüst
scheint mir dein Sinn;
in deinem Aug'
—so übermüde—
glänzt flackernde Glut.
Mit blasser Wange,
du bleiche Schwester,
was willst du Wilde von mir?

WALTRAUTE

An deiner Hand der Ring—
er ist's: hör' meinen Rat!
Für Wotan wirf ihn von dir!

BRÜNNHILDE

Den Ring—von mir?

WALTRAUTE

Den Rheintöchtern gib ihn zurück!

BRÜNNHILDE

Den Rheintöchtern—ich—den Ring?
Siegfried's Liebespfand?
Bist du von Sinnen?

WALTRAUTE

Heed with your mind what I must tell
　you!
Since you and he were parted,
he's never sent us
to the battles.
So we roam,
a wretched and leaderless troop.
As for Valhalla's heroes,
our lord shunned them.
Then, on his steed,
without let or rest,
he wandered alone through the world.
He lately came home,
holding fast in his hand
his spear in splinters.
Some hero had hacked it in pieces.
With silent signs
Wotan sent his men
to the woods,
to fell the mighty ash tree.
He bade them take
the pieces of trunk
and to pile them up high
round the great hall of the blest.
He called the gods
unto a council,
and sacredly
sat there on high.
Then he bade
the terrified ones to sit near him,
In rank and row
the hall was filled with the heroes.
There—sits he,
says no word,
upon his high seat,
still and grave,
the splintered spear
held fast in his hand.
Holda's apples
tempt not at all.
Fear and amazement
make the gods seem frozen.
Then he set both ravens
free for a journey.
If they return
with news that's welcome to hear,
once more only—
a final time—
we will perceive father smile.
Round his knees the Valkyrs
lie at his feet sadly.
Yet Wotan
is deaf to our pleading.
We're burdened by fear,
anguish and endless despair.
Upon his breast
weeping, I sorrowed.

And then he broke down.
And his thoughts were—Brünnhilde—
　you.
His eyes were closed,
he sighed deeply,
and as if dreaming,
he spoke like this:
"The day the Rhine-king's daughters
get back the ring that once they
　possessed,
marks the curse's end,
and gods and men be free."
I thought on this,
and then I left him,
through silent heroes
stealing away.
I got on my horse
in secretive haste,
and rode the storm to the rock.
Now, O sister,
I beg your help.
Bravely perform
whatever you can.
Cancel the doom of the gods.

(*She throws herself at Brünnhilde's feet.*)

BRÜNNHILDE

What whirling words are these,
what fearful and nightmarish tales!
I'm just a fool who's been banished
from the holy vapors of heaven:
I cannot grasp what you tell me.
Words like these
seem to me vain.
Within your eyes—
so heavy-weary—
gleams flicker and glow.
Your cheeks are ashen,
O pallid sister,
what wild thing is it you want?

WALTRAUTE

It's on your hand—the ring—
just that: hear my advice!
For Wotan, cast it from you!

BRÜNNHILDE

The ring—from me?

WALTRAUTE

The Rhine-daughters own it by rights!

BRÜNNHILDE

The Rhine-daughters—I—the ring?
Siegfried's pledge of love?
Have you gone crazy?

WALTRAUTE
Hör mich! hör' meine Angst!
Der Welt Unheil
haftet sicher an ihm.
Wirf ihn von dir
fort in die Welle!
Walhall's Elend zu enden,
den verfluchten wirf in die Flut!

BRÜNNHILDE
Ha! weisst du, was er mir ist?
Wie kannst du's fassen,
fühllose Maid!
Mehr als Walhall's Wonne,
mehr als der Ewigen Ruhm
ist mir der Ring:
Ein Blick auf sein helles Gold,
ein Blitz aus dem hehren Glanz
gilt mir werter
als aller Götter
ewig währendes Glück!
Denn selig aus ihm
leuchtet mir Siegfried's Liebe:
Siegfried's Liebe—
o liess' sich die Wonne dir sagen!
sie—wahrt mir der Reif.
Geh' heim zu der Götter
heiligem Rat!
Von meinem Ringe
raun' ihnen zu:
Die Liebe liesse ich nie
mir nähmen nie sie die Liebe—
stürzt auch in Trümmern
Walhall's strahlende Pracht!

WALTRAUTE
Dies deine Treue?
So in Trauer
entlässest du lieblos die Schwester?

BRÜNNHILDE
Schwinge dich fort,
fliege zu Ross!
Den Ring entführst du mir nicht!

WALTRAUTE
Wehe! Wehe!
Weh' dir, Schwester!
Wallhall's Göttern Weh!
(*Sie stürzt fort. Bald erhebt sich unter
Sturm eine Gewitterwolke aus dem
Tann, die sich bald gänzlich in der
Ferne verliert.*)

BRÜNNHILDE
Blitzend Gewölk,
Vom Wind getragen,
stürme dahin:
Zu mir nie steu're mehr her!
(*Es ist Abend geworden: aus der Tiefe
leuchtet der Feuerschein stärker auf.*)

Abendlich Dämmern
deckt den Himmel:
heller leuchtet
die hütende Lohe herauf.
Was leckt so wütend
die lodernde Welle zum Wall?
Zur Felsenspitze
wälzt sich der feurige Schwall.
(*Man hört aus der Tiefe Siegfried's
Hornruf nahen. Brünnhilde lauscht
und fährt dann entzückt auf.*)
Siegfried! . . .
Siegfried zurück!
Seinen Ruf sendet er her!
Auf! Auf! Ihm entegegen!
In meines Gottes Arm!
(*Sie stürzt in höchstem Entzücken dem
Hintergrunde zu. Feuerflammen
schlagen über den Höhensaum auf:
aus ihnen springt Siegfried auf einen
hoch ragenden Felsstein empor, wo-
rauf die Flammen wieder zurück-
weichen, und abermals nur aus der
Tiefe des Hintergrundes heraufleuch-
ten. Siegfried, auf dem Haupte den
Tarnhelm, der ihm bis zur Hälfte das
Gesicht verdeckt und nur die Augen
frei lässt, erscheint in Gunther's
Gestalt.*)

BRÜNNHILDE
(*voll Entsetzen zurückweichend*)
Verrat! Wer drang zu mir?

SIEGFRIED
(*im Hintergrunde auf dem Steine ver-
weilend, betrachtet sie lange, auf
seinen Schild gelehnt; dann redet er
sie mit verstellter Stimme an.*)
Brünnhild! Ein Freier kam,
den dein Feuer nicht geschreckt.
Dich werb' ich nun zum Weib;
du folge willig mir!

BRÜNNHILDE
Wer ist der Mann,
der das vermochte,
was dem Stärksten nur bestimmt?

SIEGFRIED
Ein Helde, der dich zähmt,
bezwingt Gewalt dich nur.

BRÜNNHILDE
(*von Grausen erfasst*)
Ein Unhold schwang sich
auf jenen Stein!
Ein Aar kam geflogen
mich zu zerfleischen!
Wer bist du, Schrecklicher?
(*Siegfried schweigt.*)
Stamm'st du von Menschen?
Kommst du von Hella's
nächtlichem Heer?

WALTRAUTE
Hear me! Heed my distress!
The world's troubles
hang right squarely on it.
Cast it from you, right in the water.
End the sorrow of Valhall,
cast the curst thing into the waves.

BRÜNNHILDE
Ha! Think now, what this would mean!
Unfeeling maid,
you do not perceive.
More than Valhall's raptures,
more than the glory of gods,
I count this ring.
A glance of its gleaming gold,
a flash of its noble light
is more precious
to me than is the lasting
luck of all the gods.
For Siegfried's dear love
blesses by shining from it.
Siegfried loves me!
Oh, might I but tell you the rapture
bound up in the ring!
Get hence to the holy
council of gods!
And of my ring
just tell them this one thing:
I never will renounce love,
nor can they keep me from loving—
rather let Valhall
crash to earth.

WALTRAUTE
This is your faith, then!
In her trouble
you coldly abandon your sister?

BRÜNNHILDE
Off on your way
Flee to your horse
I'll not abandon the ring!

WALTRAUTE
Woe's me! Woe's me!
Woe's you, sister!
Gods of Valhall, woe!

(She rushes away. Soon a stormcloud
rises from the woods with sounds of
a tempest, and quickly sails away into
the distance.)

BRÜNNHILDE
Thundering cloud,
you wind-blown bauble,
be on your way!
Storm hence and never come back!

(It is now evening. From the valley
glimmers the gradually growing fire-
light.)

Shadows of evening
shroud the heavens.
My guardian fires leap up!
The flames are raging,
and licking their tongues to the wall.
The fiery tide
rolls up to the peak of the rock.
(She starts in rapture.)
Siegfried!
Siegfried is back?
It is he sending his call.
Up! Up, to be gathered
into my god's embrace!
(She hastens joyfully to the edge of the
crag. Flames leap up, out of which
Siegfried springs forward onto a high
rock, whereupon the flames immediately withdraw and again only shine
up from below. Brünnhilde recoils,
flies to the foreground, and from
there, in speechless astonishment,
stares at Siegfried, who has appeared
in Gunther's form, wearing the Tarnhelm, whose visor covers half his face,
leaving only the eyes free.)

BRÜNNHILDE
(retreating in horror)
Betrayed! What man are you?

SIEGFRIED
(remaining on the rock, motionless and
leaning on his shield as he gazes at
her. He speaks harshly.)
Brünnhilde, your wooer comes,
one who's fearless of the fire.
I've come here for a wife.
So follow where I lead.

BRÜNNHILDE
Who is the man
who has achieved that
which the strongest only can?

SIEGFRIED
A hero, who'll be tamed
when once you yield your might.

BRÜNNHILDE
(terrified)
A demon's climbed
to this rocky peak.
An eagle has flown here
to tear me to bits!
Who are you, dreadful one?
(Siegfried is silent.)
Are you a human?
Are you of Hella's
hosts of the night?

SIEGFRIED

Ein Gibichung bin ich,
und Gunther heisst der Held,
dem, Frau, du folgen sollst.

BRÜNNHILDE

(*in Verzweiflung ausbrechend*)

Wotan! ergrimmter,
grausamer Gott!
Weh'! nun erseh' ich
der Strafe Sinn:
Zu Hohn und Jammer
jagst du mich hin!

SIEGFRIED

(*springt vom Stein herab und tritt
näher*)

Die Nacht bricht an:
in deinem Gemach
musst du dich mir vermählen!

BRÜNNHILDE

(*den Finger, an dem sie Siegfried's Ring
trägt, drohend emporstreckend*)

Bleib' fern! fürchte dies Zeichen!
Zur Schande zwingst du mich nicht,
solang' der Ring mich beschützt.

SIEGFRIED

Mannersrecht gebe er Gunther:
durch den Ring sei ihm vermählt!

BRÜNNHILDE

Zurück, du Räuber!
Frevelnder Dieb!
Erfreche dich nicht mir zu nah'n!
Stärker als Stahl
macht mich der Ring:
nie—raubst du ihn mir!

SIEGFRIED

Von dir ihn zu lösen
lehrst du mich nun.

(*Er dringt auf sie ein; sie ringen.
Brünnhilde windet sich los und flieht.
Siegfried setzt ihr nach. Sie ringen
von Neuem: er erfasst sie, und
entzieht ihrem Finger den Ring. Sie
schreit laut auf und sinkt, wie zer-
brochen, auf der Steinbank vor dem
Gemach zusammen.*)

Jetzt bist du mein!
Brünnhilde, Gunther's Braut—
gönne mir nun dein Gemach!

BRÜNNHILDE

(*fast ohnmächtig*)

Was könntest du wehren,

elendes Weib?

(*Siegfried treibt sie mit einer gebieten-
den Bewegung an: zitternd und
wankenden Schrittes geht sie in das
Gemach.*)

SIEGFRIED

(*das Schwert ziehend*)

Nun, Notung zeuge du,
dass ich in Züchten warb.
Die Treue wahrend dem Bruder,
trenne mich von seiner Braut!

(*Er folgt Brünnhilde nach.*)

ZWEITER AUFZUG

Uferraum

*Vor der Halle der Gibichungen: rechts
der offene Eingang zur Halle; links
das Rheinufer. Von diesem aus
erhebt sich eine durch verschiedene
Bergpfade gespaltene, felsige Anhöhe,
quer über die Bühne, nach rechts
dem Hintergrunde zu aufsteigend.
Dort sieht man einen der Fricka
errichteten Weihstein welchem,
höher hinauf, ein grösserer für Wotan, sowie seitwärts ein gleicher, für
Donner geweihter, entspricht. Es ist
Nacht.*

(*Hagen, den Speer im Arm, den Schild
zur Seite, sitzt schlafend in der Halle.
Der Mond wirft plötzlich ein grelles
Licht auf ihn und seine nächste Um-
gebung: man gewahrt Alberich vor
Hagen kauernd, die Arme auf dessen
Knie gelehnt.*)

ALBERICH

(*leise*)

Schläfst du, Hagen, mein Sohn?
Du schläfst, und hörst mich nicht,
den Ruh' und Schlaf verriet?

HAGEN

(*leise, und ohne sich zu rühren*)

Ich höre dich, schlimmer Albe:
was hast du meinem Schlaf zu sagen?

ALBERICH

Gemahnt sei der Macht,
der du gebietest,
bist du so mutig,
wie die Mutter dich mir gebar!

HAGEN

Gab die Mutter mir Mut,
nicht mag ich ihr doch danken,
dass deiner List sie erlag:
frühalt, fahl und bleich,
hass' ich die Frohen,
freue mich nie!

SIEGFRIED

A Gibichung am I,
and Gunther is my name,
whom, maid, you'll follow now.

BRÜNNHILDE

(in an outburst of despair)

Wotan! you grim
and terrible god!
Woe! Now I fathom
your wrathful curse!
My shame and sorrow
come from your will.

SIEGFRIED

(leaping from the rock and approaching)

The night has come,
I ask for your room,
you must be mine for marriage.

BRÜNNHILDE

(threateningly stretching out her finger
on which is Siegfried's ring)

Stand back! Flee from this token!
You cannot take me by force,
while yet this ring stands on guard.

SIEGFRIED

This is a token for Gunther:
he will wed you with this ring.

BRÜNNHILDE

Go back, you robber!
Villainous thief!
Don't venture, you rogue, to come
near!
This is my strength,
stronger than steel.
This—cannot be robbed!

SIEGFRIED

Why then you shall teach me
how it is mine.

(He presses toward her. They struggle.
Brünnhilde tears herself free and flees.
Siegfried pursues her. Again they
struggle. He seizes her and plucks the
ring from her finger. She utters a
loud scream and sinks exhausted on
the rocky seat in front of the cave.)

Now you are mine!
Brünnhilde, Gunther's bride.
Go with me now to your room.

BRÜNNHILDE

(almost fainting)

Most wretched of women,

what help do I have?

(Siegfried drives her in commandingly.
She goes into the cave, trembling,
and with tottering steps.)

SIEGFRIED

(drawing his sword)

Now, Needful, witness here,
that I have chastely wooed,
and kept my oath to my brother.
Serve as wall between us two.

(He follows Brünnhilde.)

ACT TWO

A River Bank

Before the hall of the Gibichungs: to
the right the open entrance to the
hall, to the left the bank of the
Rhine. From the latter, mounting
toward the back, rises a rocky height,
cut by several mountain paths. There
an altar-stone to Fricka is visible, as
well as one, higher up, to Wotan,
and one at the side to Donner. It is
night. Hagen, spear in hand and
shield at side, sits sleeping against the
hall. The moon suddenly throws a
keen light on him and his surround-
ings: Alberich is seen crouching in
front of him, leaving his arms on
Hagen's knees.

ALBERICH

(softly)

Sleeping, Hagen, my son?
You sleep and hear not him
whom rest and sleep forsake?

HAGEN

(softly and without moving)

I hear you well, harassed elfin.
What is it I should know while sleeping?

ALBERICH

Remember the might
you are endowed with—
if you've the courage
that your mother gave you at birth.

HAGEN

My courage came from her,
and yet I cannot thank her
that she succumbed to your spell.
Wizened, wan and pale,
I hate the happy,
never rejoice.

ALBERICH

Hagen, mein Sohn,
hasse die Frohen!
Mich Lust-freien,
Leid-belasteten,
liebst du so wie du sollst!
Bist du kräftig,
kühn und klug:
die wir bekämpfen
mit nächtigem Krieg,
schon gibt ihnen Not unser Neid.
Der einst den Ring mir entriss,
Wotan, der wütende Räuber,
vom eig'nen Geschlechte
ward er geschlagen:
an den Wälsung verlor er
Macht und Gewalt;
mit der Götter ganzer Sippe
in Angst ersieht er sein Ende.
Nicht ihn fürcht' ich mehr:
fallen muss er mit Allen!
Schläfst du, Hagen, mein Sohn?

HAGEN
(bleibt unverändert wie zuvor)
Der Ewigen Macht,
wer erbte sie?

ALBERICH
Ich—und du:
wir erben die Welt,
trüg' ich mich nicht
in deiner Treu',
teil'st du meinen Gram und Grimm.
Wotan's Speer
zerspellte der Wälsung,
der Fafner, den Wurm,
im Kampfe gefällt,
und kindisch den Reif sich errang:
Jede Gewalt
hat er gewonnen;
Walhall und Nibelheim
neigen sich ihm.
An dem furchtlosen Helden
erlahmt selbst mein Fluch;
denn nicht kennt er
des Ringes Wert,
zu nichts nützt er
die neidlichste Macht.
Lachend in liebender Brunst
brennt er lebend dahin.
Ihn zu verderben
taugt uns nun einzig . . .
Schläfst du, Hagen, mein Sohn?

HAGEN
(wie zuvor)
Zu seinem Verderben
dient er mir schon.

ALBERICH
Den gold'nen Ring,
den Reif gilt's zu erringen!
Ein weises Weib
lebt dem Wälsung zu Lieb':
Riet es ihm je
des Rheines Töchtern
—die in Wassers Tiefen
einst mich betört!—
zurück zu geben den Ring:
verloren ging mir das Gold:
keine List erlangte es je.
Drum ohne Zögern
ziel' auf den Reif!
Dich Zaglosen
zeugt' ich mir ja,
dass wider Helden
hart du mir hieltest.
Zwar stark nicht genug
den Wurm zu besteh'n
—was allein dem Wälsung bestimmt—
zu zähem Hass doch
erzog ich Hagen;
der soll mich nun rächen,
den Ring gewinnen,
dem Wälsung und Wotan zum Hohn!
Schwörst du mir's, Hagen, mein Sohn?

HAGEN
Den Ring soll ich haben,
harre in Ruh'!

ALBERICH
Schwörst du mir's, Hagen, mein Held?

HAGEN
Mir selbst schwör' ich's:
schweige die Sorge!
(Ein immer finsterer Schatten bedeckt
wieder Hagen und Alberich: vom
Rhein her dämmert der Tag.)

ALBERICH
(wie er allmählich immer mehr dem
Blicke entschwindet, wird auch seine
Stimme immer unvernehmbarer.)
Sei treu, Hagen, mein Sohn!
Trauter Helde, sei treu!
Sei treu! treu!

(Alberich ist gänzlich verschwunden.
Hagen, der unverrückt in seiner Stel-
lung verblieben, blickt regungslos und
starren Auges nach dem Rheine hin.)
(Die Sonne geht auf und spiegelt sich
in der Flut.)
(Siegfried tritt plötzlich, dicht am
Ufer, hinter einem Busche hervor.
Er ist in seiner eigenen Gestalt; nur
den Tarnhelm hat er noch auf dem
Haupte: er zieht ihn ab, und hängt
ihn an den Gürtel.)

ALBERICH

Hagen, my son,
hate all the happy,
but love as you should
the one who's so sad
and burdened with care.
If you are hardy,
bold and smart,
those whom we strive with
in conflict by night
will soon bear the marks of our spite.
The one who once seized my ring,
Wotan, the ravening robber,
at last has been vanquished
by his own offspring.
Through the Volsung he's lost
his power and might.
With the gods assembled round him
he waits his downfall in anguish.
My fear now has gone:
he will perish among them.
Sleeping, Hagen, my son?

HAGEN

(still motionless)

Who's heir to the might
of gods above?

ALBERICH

I—and you:
we're heirs of the world,
if I can count
upon your faith,
sharing both my woe and wrath.
Wotan's spear
was split by the Volsung.
And through his great might
the dragon was slain.
He playfully picked up the ring.
Now he is lord of every power.
Valhall and Nibelhome
bow to his might.
Since this hero is fearless
my curses are lame.
He knows not how the ring is used,
he knows not its murderous might.
Laughter and love fill his heart:
joy in living is his.
Now we must plot
just how to destroy him.
Sleeping, Hagen, my son?

HAGEN

(as before)

Already I've helped him
toward his doom.

ALBERICH

The golden ring—
the ring—that we must capture.
A cunning, wise woman
lives for his love:
if she advise
that he return it
to the waters where
the Rhine-maidens live—
those girls who made me a fool—
the circlet then will be lost;
and no art will win it again.
Therefore delay not,
aim for the ring.
I bred you
as one without fear,
so you could fight my foes
when I needed.
True, you were not strong
enough for that foe
which the Volsung slaughtered with
    ease.
I brought up Hagen
to live in hate,
and this son shall avenge me,
and win the circlet—
then Volsung and Wotan are doomed!
Swear to me, Hagen, my son?

HAGEN

The ring shall be ravished:
rest now in peace.

ALBERICH

Swear to me, Hagen, my son?

HAGEN

My heart swears it.
Silence your sorrow.

(An increasing gloom hides Hagen and
    Alberich. Day is arriving on the
    Rhine.)

ALBERICH

(his voice fainter and fainter)

Be true, Hagen, my son,
trusty hero, be true.
Be true—true!

(He vanishes completely. Hagen stares
    fixedly upon the Rhine. The sun
    rises and is mirrored in the waters.
    Suddenly Siegfried comes forward
    from behind a bush on the river bank.
    He bears his own form, but the
    Tarnhelm is still on his head. He
    takes this off as he advances, and
    hangs it on his girdle.)

SIEGFRIED

Hoiho! Hagen!
Müder Mann!
Siehst du mich kommen?

HAGEN
(gemächlich sich erhebend)

Hei! Siegfried!
Geschwinder Helde!
Wo brausest du her?

SIEGFRIED

Vom Brünnhildenstein;
dort sog ich den Atem ein,
mit dem ich dich rief:
So rasch war meine Fahrt!
Langsamer folgt mir ein Paar:
Zu Schiff gelangt das her.

HAGEN

So zwangst du Brünnhild'?

SIEGFRIED

Wacht Gutrune?

HAGEN
(in die Halle rufend)

Hoiho! Gutrune!
Komm' heraus!
Siegfried ist da:
was säumst du drin?

SIEGFRIED
(zur Halle sich wendend)

Euch beiden meld' ich,
wie ich Brünnhild' band.
(Gutrune tritt ihm aus der Halle
entgegen.)
Heiss' mich willkommen,
Gibichskind!
Ein guter Bote bin ich dir.

GUTRUNE

Freia grüsse dich
zu aller Frauen Ehre!

SIEGFRIED

Frei und hold
sei nun mir Frohem:
Zum Weib gewann ich dich heut'.

GUTRUNE

So folgt Brünnhild' meinem Bruder?

SIEGFRIED

Leicht ward die Frau ihm gefreit.

GUTRUNE

Sengte das Feuer ihn nicht?

SIEGFRIED

Ihn hätt' es auch nicht versehrt;
doch ich durchschritt es für ihn,
da dich ich wollt' erwerben.

GUTRUNE

Und dich hat es verschont?

SIEGFRIED

Mich freute die schwebende Brunst.

GUTRUNE

Hielt Brünnhild' dich für Gunther?

SIEGFRIED

Ihm glich ich auf das Haar:
Der Tarnhelm wirkte das,
wie Hagen tüchtig es wies.

HAGEN

Dir gab ich guten Rat.

GUTRUNE

So zwangst du das kühne Weib?

SIEGFRIED

Sie wich—Gunther's Kraft.

GUTRUNE

Und vermählte sie sich dir?

SIEGFRIED

Ihrem Mann gehorchte Brünhild'
eine volle bräutliche Nacht.

GUTRUNE

Als ihr Mann doch galtest du?

SIEGFRIED

Bei Gutrune weilte Siegfried.

GUTRUNE

Doch zur Seite war ihm Brünhild'?

SIEGFRIED

Zwischen Ost und West der Nord:
so nah' war Brünnhild' ihm fern.

GUTRUNE

Wie empfing Gunther sie nun von
dir?

SIEGFRIED

Durch des Feuers verlöschende Lohe
im Frühnebel vom Felsen
folgte sie mir zu Tal;
dem Strande nah,
flugs die Stelle
tauschte Gunther mit mir.
Durch des Geschmeides Tugend
wünscht' ich mich schnell hieher.
Ein starker Wind nun treibt
die Trauten den Rhein herauf:
d'rum rüstet jetzt den Empfang!

SIEGFRIED

Hoiho! Hagen!
Weary man!
How did I get here?

HAGEN

(rising indolently)

Hey! Siegfried!
Most speedy hero!
Where were you till now?

SIEGFRIED

At Brünnhilde's rock;
and there I drew in that breath
I spent when I called:
so fast was my exploit.
Two that are coming, must lag.
A boat now bears them here.

HAGEN

You mastered Brünnhilde?

SIEGFRIED

Where's Gutrune?

HAGEN

(calling toward the hall)

Hoiho! Gutrune!
Come on out!
Siegfried is here;
why stay inside?

SIEGFRIED

(turning toward the hall)

I'll tell you both
the way I bound Brünnhilde.
(Gutrune approaches him from the
hall.)
Now bid me welcome,
Gibich child.
I come to you with happy news.

GUTRUNE

Freia give you joy,
to every woman's honor!

SIEGFRIED

Freely grant me
joy and favor!
This day has made you my wife.

GUTRUNE

Does Brünnhilde come with my
   brother?

SIEGFRIED

Soon did he win what he wished.

GUTRUNE

Was he not singed by the fire?

SIEGFRIED

No, it would not have done harm,
and yet I stepped through for him,
to win the prize of Gutrune!

GUTRUNE

You went right through unscathed?

SIEGFRIED

The flickering fire was fun!

GUTRUNE

Did Brünnhilde think you Gunther?

SIEGFRIED

We looked as like as hairs.
The Tarnhelm did the trick,
as Hagen told me it would.

HAGEN

I gave you good advice.

GUTRUNE

You mastered the valiant maid?

SIEGFRIED

She felt Gunther's might.

GUTRUNE

Was she married then to you?

SIEGFRIED

She obeyed her rightful husband
for a full and marital night.

GUTRUNE

Did you pass as rightful spouse?

SIEGFRIED

The one I await is Gutrune.

GUTRUNE

Yet did Brünnhilde lie beside him?

SIEGFRIED

East and West are near the North;
So near was Brünnhilde, so far.

GUTRUNE

How then did Gunther obtain the
   bride?

SIEGFRIED

Through the flames that were flickering
   and dying,
Through morn's mists from the rock
she followed me down the vale.
And near the shore
I and Gunther
made exchange of our forms:
Then, through the helmet's virtue,
flash, I am straightway here.
A driving wind now brings
the dear ones right up the Rhine.
So greet them well when they come!

GUTRUNE
Siegfried, mächtigster Mann:
wie fasst mich Furcht vor dir!

HAGEN
(*von der Höhe im Hintergrunde den
Fluss hinab spähend*)
In der Ferne seh' ich ein Segel.

SIEGFRIED
So sagt dem Boten Dank!

GUTRUNE
Lasst uns sie hold empfangen,
dass heiter sie und gern hier weile!
Du Hagen! Minnig
rufe die Mannen
nach Gibich's Hof zur Hochzeit!
Frohe Frauen
ruf' ich zum Fest:
der Freudigen folgen sie gern.
(*nach der Halle schreitend, zu Siegfried*)
Rastest du, schlimmer Held?

SIEGFRIED
Dir zu helfen ruh' ich aus.
(*Er folgt ihr. Beide gehen in die Halle
ab.*)

HAGEN
(*auf der Anhöhe stehend, stösst, der
Landseite zugewendet, mit aller
Kraft in ein grosses Stierhorn*)
Hoiho, Hoiho! Hoiho!
Ihr Gibich's-Mannen,
machet euch auf!
Wehe! Wehe!
Waffen! Waffen!
Waffen durch's Land!
Gute Waffen!
Starke Waffen!
Scharf zum Streit!
Not ist da!
Not! Wehe! Wehe!
Hoiho! Hoiho! Hoho!
(*Er bläst abermals. Aus verschiedenen
Gegenden vom Lande her antworten
Heerhörner. Von den Höhen und aus
dem Tale stürmen in Hast und Eile
gewaffnete Mannen herbei.*)

DIE MANNEN
(*erst einzelne, dann immer mehrere zu-
sammen*)
Was tost das Horn?
Was ruft es zu Heer?
Wir kommen mit Wehr,
Wir kommen mit Waffen,
mit starken Waffen,
mit scharfer Wehr!
Hoiho! Hoiho.

Hagen! Hagen!
Welche Not ist da?
Welcher Feind ist nah?
Wer gibt uns Streit?
Ist Gunther in Not?

HAGEN
Rüstet euch wohl
und rastet nicht;
Gunther sollt' ihr empfah'n:
Ein Weib hat der gefreit.

DIE MANNEN
Drohet ihm Not?
Drängt ihn der Feind?

HAGEN
Ein freisliches Weib
führt er heim.

DIE MANNEN
Ihm folgen der Magen
feindliche Mannen?

HAGEN
Einsam fährt er:
Keiner folgt.

DIE MANNEN
So bestand er die Not,
bestand den Kampf?

HAGEN
Der Wurmtöter wehrte die Not:
Siegfried, der Held, der schuf ihm Heil.

DIE MANNEN
Was soll ihm das Heer nun noch helfen?

HAGEN
Starke Stiere
sollt ihr schlachten:
am Weihstein fliesse
Wotan ihr Blut.

DIE MANNEN
Was, Hagen, was hiessest du uns dann?

HAGEN
Einen Eber fällen
sollt ihr für Froh;
einen stämmigen Bock
stechen für Donner;
Schafe aber
schlachtet für Fricka,
dass gute Ehe sie gebe!

DIE MANNEN
(*mit immer mehr ausbrechender Hei-
terkeit*)
Schlugen wir Tiere,
was schaffen wir dann?

GUTRUNE

Siegfried, masterful man,
I feel afraid of you!

HAGEN

(calling from the shore)

I can see a sail in the distance!

SIEGFRIED

So give the herald thanks!

GUTRUNE

Let her have a gracious welcome
to please her so she'll love to tarry.
You Hagen! gaily
summon the vassals
to Gibich's court for wedding,
while I call the maids to the feast.
They'll merrily join in the fun!

(As she goes toward the hall she turns
round again.)

Man of war, won't you rest?

SIEGFRIED

Just to help you gives me rest.

(He follows her. Both go into the hall.)

HAGEN

(standing on a rock at the back, starts
blowing his cow-horn)

Hoiho! Hoiho! Hoiho!
You men of Gibich!
Get yourselves up!
Waken! Waken!

Weapons! Weapons!
Arm through the land!
Go dry weapons!
Mighty weapons!
Sharp for strife!
Foes are here!
Foes! Waken!
Hoiho! Hoihohoho!

(Hagen remains on his station. Other
horns answer his from different direc-
tions. From the heights and valleys
armed men rush on.)

THE VASSALS

(a few first, then gradually increasing
in number)

Why blares the horn?
What calls us to war?
We come with our arms,
we come with our weapons,
with mighty weapons,
with keenest arms!
Hoiho! Hoiho!

Hagen! Hagen!
What's the danger here?
Who's the foe that's near?
Who comes to fight?
Is Gunther in need?

HAGEN

Ready yourselves
and waste no time.
Gunther soon will be here.
Your lord comes with a bride.

THE MEN

What is his need?
Who is it threats?

HAGEN

He's bringing a wife
fiery and proud.

THE MEN

Do furious kinsfolk
follow for vengeance?

HAGEN

No one follows.
He's alone.

THE MEN

Has he righted a wrong
and conquered in war?

HAGEN

The dragon-destroyer gave aid:
Siegfried the brave gave mighty help!

THE MEN

Then what is the need of our army?

HAGEN

Steers of value
must be slaughtered,
and Wotan's altar
must flow with their blood.

THE MEN

Why, Hagen, what would you have us
do?

HAGEN

Let a boar be slaughtered:
Thus honor Froh.
Get a vigorous goat,
slay it for Donner.
Sheep must then be
slaughtered for Fricka,
to gain her blessing in wedlock.

THE MEN

(with ever-increasing mirth)

When we have slain them,
what then shall we do?

HAGEN
Das Trinkhorn nehmt
von trauten Frau'n,
mit Met und Wein
wonnig gefüllt.

DIE MANNEN
Das Trinkhorn zur Hand,
wie halten wir es dann?

HAGEN
Rüstig gezecht,
bis der Rausch euch zähmt:
alles den Göttern zu Ehren,
das gute Ehe sie geben!

DIE MANNEN
(in ein schallendes Gelächter ausbrechend)
Gross Glück und Heil
lacht nun dem Rhein,
da Hagen, der Grimme,
so lustig mag sein!
Der Hagedorn
sticht nun nicht mehr:
Zum Hochzeitsrufer
ward er bestellt.

HAGEN
(der immer ernst geblieben)
Nun lasst das Lachen,
mut'ge Mannen!
Empfangt Gunther's Braut:
Brünnhilde naht dort mit ihm.
(Er ist herabgestiegen und unter die
Mannen getreten. Er deutet die Mannen nach dem Rhein hin: diese eilen
zum Teil auf die Anhöhe, während
andere sich am Ufer aufstellen.)
Hold seid der Herrin,
helfet ihr treu:
traf sie ein Leid,
rasch seid zur Rache!
(Gunther und Brünnhilde sind im
Nachen angekommen. Einige der
Mannen springen in den Fluss, und
ziehen den Kahn an das Land. Während Gunther Brünnhilde an das
Ufer geleitet, schlagen die Mannen
jauchzend an die Waffen. Hagen
steht zur Seite im Hintergrunde.)

DIE MANNEN
Heil! Heil!
Willkommen! Willkommen!
Heil dir, Gunther!
Heil deiner Braut!

GUNTHER
(Brünnhilde, welche bleich und gesenk-
ten Blickes ihm folgt, den Mannen
vorstellend)
Brünnhild', die hehrste Frau,

bring ich euch her zum Rhein:
ein edleres Weib
ward nie gewonnen.
Der Gibichungen Geschlecht,
gaben die Götter ihm Gunst,
zum höchsten Ruhm
rag' es nun auf!

DIE MANNEN
Heil! Heil dir, Gunther!
Glücklicher Gibichung!
(Brünnhilde folgt Gunther, der sie zur
Halle führt, aus welcher jetzt Sieg-
fried und Gutrune, von Frauen be-
gleitet, heraustreten.)

GUNTHER
Gegrüsst sei, teurer Held,
gegrüsst, holde Schwester!
Dich seh' ich froh ihm zur Seite,
der dich zum Weib gewann.
Zwei sel'ge Paare
seh' ich hier prangen:
Brünnhild' und Gunther,
Gutrun' und Siegfried!
(Brünnhilde erschrickt, schlägt die Augen auf, und erblickt Siegfried: sie
lässt Gunther's Hand fahren, geht
heftig bewegt einen Schritt auf Siegfried zu, weicht entsetzt zurük, und
heftet starr den Blick auf ihn. Alle
sind sehr betroffen.)

MANNEN UND FRAUEN
Was ist ihr?
Ist sie entrückt?

SIEGFRIED
Was müh't Brünnhilde's Blick?

BRÜNNHILDE
(kaum ihrer mächtig)
Siegfried . . . hier! Gutrune . . . ?

SIEGFRIED
Gunther's milde Schwester:
mir vermählt,
wie Gunther du.

BRÜNNHILDE
Ich . . . Gunther . . . ? Du lügst!
Mir schwindet das Licht . . .
(Sie droht umzusinken: Siegfried, ihr
zunächst, stützt sie.)
Siegfried . . . kennt mich nicht?

SIEGFRIED
Gunther, deinem Weib ist übel!
(Gunther tritt hinzu.)
Erwache, Frau!
Hier steht dein Gatte.
(Indem Siegfried auf Gunther mit
dem Finger deutet, erkennt an diesem
Brünnhilde den Ring.)

HAGEN

You'll take the cup
from lovely maids,
and down the drinks
of mead and of wine!

THE MEN

The cup in our hands,
what then are we to do?

HAGEN

Revel away
till your wits are wet.
Thus you will honor the gods
and they will then prosper the marriage!

THE MEN

(*with ringing peals of laughter*)

Great luck now smiles
here on the Rhine,
when Hagen, the grim one,
indulges in mirth!
The prickly thorn
prickles no more!
A wedding-helper
let him be called!

HAGEN (*quite serious*)

Now leave off laughing,
valiant vassals!
Receive Gunther's bride:
Brünnhilde nears now with him.

(*He descends and joins the men. He
orders them toward the Rhine. Some
hasten to the heights, others to the
banks.*)

Honor your mistress,
pledge her your truth;
if she is wronged
haste to avenge her.

(*Gunther and Brünnhilde arrive in
the boat. Some of the men spring
into the water and drag the boat
ashore. While Gunther conducts
Brünnhilde ashore, the men shout
and clash their weapons. Hagen
stands off.*)

THE MEN

Hail! Hail!
We greet you! Be welcome!
Hail, O Gunther!
Hail to your bride!

GUNTHER

(*presenting Brünnhilde, who follows
him with pale and downcast looks*)

Brünnhilde, most queenly bride

comes with me to our shores.
No man ever won
a nobler woman.
The Gibichungs' lofty race
received the favor of gods.
Their highest fame
now has arrived.

THE MEN

Hail! Hail to you, Gunther!
Fortunate Gibichung!

(*Gunther leads Brünnhilde toward the
hall, from which Siegfried and Gutrune, attended by women, step
forth.*)

GUNTHER

All hail, most valiant man!
All hail, lovely sister!
I joy to see you beside him.
who won you for his bride.
Two blessed couples,
glowing and radiant,
Brünnhilde—and Gunther,
Gutrune—and Siegfried!

(*Brünnhilde startled, raises her eyes
and perceives Siegfried. She drops
Gunther's hand, steps toward Siegfried, then recoils in horror and
glares at him. All are wonder-
struck.*)

MEN, WOMEN

What ails her?
Is she distraught?

SIEGFRIED

What clouds Brünnhilde's look?

BRÜNNHILDE

(*almost swooning*)

Siegfried . . . here . . . ! Gutrune . . . ?

SIEGFRIED

Gunther's gentle sister.
She's my bride,
as you are his.

BRÜNNHILDE

I . . . Gunther . . . ? You lie!
The light has gone out!

(*She nearly falls. Siegfried supports
her.*)

Siegfried . . . knows me not?

SIEGFRIED

Gunther, see, your wife is ailing!

(*Gunther steps over to her.*)

Awaken, wife,
here is your husband!

(*As Siegfried points to Gunther, Brünnhilde perceives the ring on his
finger.*)

BRÜNNHILDE
(*mit furchtbarer Heftigkeit aufschreck-
end*)
Ha! der Ring . . .
an seiner Hand!
Er . . . Siegfried?

MANNEN UND FRAUEN
Was ist?

HAGEN
(*aus dem Hintergrunde unter die Mannen tretend*)
Jetzt merket klug,
was die Frau euch klagt!

BRÜNNHILDE
(*sich ermannend, indem sie die schreck-
lichste Aufregung gewaltsam zurück-
hält*)
Einen Ring sah ich
an deiner Hand:
nicht dir gehört er,
ihn entriss mir
          (*auf Gunther deutend*)
—dieser Mann!
Wie mochtest von ihm
den Ring du empfah'n?

SIEGFRIED
(*aufmerksam den Ring an seiner Hand
betrachtend*)
Den Ring empfing ich nicht von ihm.

BRÜNNHILDE (*zu Gunther*)
Nahmst du von mir den Ring,
durch den ich dir vermählt;
so melde ihm dein Recht,
ford're zurück das Pfand!

GUNTHER
          (*in grosser Verwirrung*)
Den Ring? Ich gab ihm keinen:
Doch kennst du ihn auch gut?

BRÜNNHILDE
Wo bärgest du den Ring,
den du von mir erbeutet?
(*Gunther schweigt in höchster Betrof-
fenheit.*)
Ha! Dieser war es,
der mir den Ring entriss:
Siegfried, der trugvolle Dieb!

SIEGFRIED
(*der über der Betrachtung des Ringes
in fernes Sinnen entrückt war*)
Von keinem Weib
kam mir der Reif;
noch war's ein Weib,
dem ich ihn abgewann:
Genau erkenn' ich
des Kampfes Lohn,
den vor Neidhöhl' einst ich bestand,
als den starken Wurm ich erschlug.

HAGEN
          (*zwischen sie tretend*)
Brünnhild', kühne Frau!
Kennst du genau den Ring?
Ist's der, den du Gunther'n gabst,
so ist er sein,
und Siegfried gewann ihn durch Trug,
den der Treulose büssen sollt'!

BRÜNNHILDE
(*in furchtbarstem Schmerz aufschrei-
end*)
Betrug! Betrug!
Schändlichster Betrug!
Verrat! Verrat!
Wie noch nie er gerächt!

GUTRUNE
Verrat! An wem?

MANNEN UND FRAUEN
An wem Verrat?

BRÜNNHILDE
Heilige Götter!
Himmlische Lenker!
Rauntet ihr dies
in eurem Rat?
Lehrt ihr mich Leiden
wie keiner sie litt?
Schuft ihr mir Schmach
wie nie sie geschmerzt?
Ratet nun Rache
wie nie sie gerast!
Zündet mir Zorn
wie noch nie er gezähmt!
Heisset Brünnhild'
ihr Herz zu zerbrechen,
den zu zertrümmern,
der sie betrog!

GUNTHER
Brünnhild', Gemahlin!
Mäss'ge dich!

BRÜNNHILDE
Weich' fern, Verräter!
selbst Verrat'ner!
Wisset denn Alle:
nicht ihm,
dem Manne dort
bin ich vermählt.

MANNEN UND FRAUEN
Siegfried? Gutrun's Gemahl?

BRÜNNHILDE
Er zwang mir Lust
und Liebe ab.

BRUNNHILDE

(*with a fearful start*)

Ha—the ring
upon his hand.
He . . . Siegfried?

MEN, WOMEN

What's wrong?

HAGEN (*advancing*)

Now listen well
to the woman's plaint.

BRÜNNHILDE

(*trying to control her emotion*)

On your hand there
I beheld a ring:
you do now own it,
it was ravished—
                    (*pointing to Gunther*)
by this man.
But how did the ring
come into your hands?

SIEGFRIED

(*attentively studying the ring on his finger*)

This ring—it did not
come from him.

BRÜNNHILDE (*to Gunther*)

If it was you who seized
this ring that made us one,
assert your rightful claim:
get back your pledge again.

GUNTHER (*perplexed*)

The ring—I did not give it.
You, though, must know him well.

BRÜNNHILDE

Where have you kept the ring
that I was forced to give you?
(*Gunther, bewildered, remains silent.*)
Ha! Here's the man!
This is he who took my ring:
Siegfried, the treacherous thief!

SIEGFRIED

(*absorbed in contemplation of the ring*)

No woman, sure,
gave me this ring,
nor was it torn
from off a woman's hand.
I know it well
as a prize of strife
which I won at the hate-cavern once
when I slew the dragon on guard.

HAGEN

(*stepping between them*)

Brünnhilde, valiant wife!
Say if you know this ring.
If you gave it to your spouse,
then it is his,
and Siegfried obtained it through guile,
and the traitor must pay for the theft.

BRÜNNHILDE

(*shrieking in anguish*)

Deceit! Deceit!
Dastardly deceit!
Betrayed! Betrayed!
Wrong too black for revenge!

GUTRUNE

Deceit?

MEN, WOMEN

But who's betrayed?

BRÜNNHILDE

Gods immortal!
Heavenly leaders!
Did your decrees
include such woe?
Grief you have taught me
as none ever knew,
painfullest shame
unfelt till this hour!
Grant me such vengeance
as never was known!
Kindle a wrath
that can never be quenched!
Order Brünnhilde's
poor heart to be shattered,
if he who wronged her
may be destroyed!

GUNTHER

Brünnhilde, beloved,
calm yourself!

BRÜNNHILDE

Away, betrayer!
Yes—betrayed one!
All of you, listen!
Not he—
but—that one there—
he is my spouse.

MEN, WOMEN

Siegfried? Gutrune's spouse?

BRÜNNHILDE

He forced delight
and love from me.

SIEGFRIED

Achtest du so
der eig'nen Ehre?
Die Zunge, die sie lästert,
muss ich der Lüge sie zeihen?
Hört, ob ich Treue brach!
Blutbrüderschaft
hab' ich Gunther geschworen;
Notung, das werte Schwert,
wahrte der Treue Eid;
mich trennte seine Schärfe
von diesem traurigen Weib.

BRÜNNHILDE

Du listiger Held,
sieh' wie du lügst!
wie auf dein Schwert
du schlecht dich berufst!
Wohl kenn' ich seine Schärfe,
doch kenn' auch die Scheide,
darin so wonnig
ruht' an der Wand
Notung, der treue Freund,
als die Traute sein Herr sich gefreit.

DIE MANNEN

(in lebhafter Entrüstung zusammentre-
tend)

Wie? Brach er die Treue?
Trübte er Gunther's Ehre?

GUNTHER

Geschändet wär' ich,
schmählich bewahrt,
gäb'st du die Rede
nicht ihr zurück!

GUTRUNE

Treulos, Siegfried,
sannest du Trug?
Bezeuge, dass jene
falsch dich zeiht!

DIE MANNEN

Reinige dich,
bist du im Recht:
schweige die Klage,
schwöre den Eid!

SIEGFRIED

Schweig' ich die Klage,
schwör' ich den Eid:
wer von euch wagt
seine Waffe daran?

HAGEN

Meines Speeres Spitze
wag' ich daran:
sie wahr' in Ehren den Eid.

(Die Mannen schliessen einen Ring um
Hagen und Siegfried; Hagen hält
diesem die Spitze seines Speeres hin:
Siegfried legt zwei Finger seiner
rechten Hand darauf.)

SIEGFRIED

Helle Wehr!
Heilige Waffe!
Hilf meinem ewigen Eide!
Bei des Speeres Spitze
sprech' ich den Eid:
Spitze, achte des Spruchs!
Wo Scharfes mich schneidet,
schneide du mich;
wo der Tod mich soll treffen,
treffe du mich:
Klagte das Weib dort wahr,
brach ich dem Bruder die Treu'!

BRÜNNHILDE

(tritt wütend in den Ring, reisst Siegfried's Hand vom Speere, und fasst
dafür mit der ihrigen die Spitze)

Helle Wehr!
Heilige Waffe!
Hilf meinem ewigen Eide!
Bei des Speeres Spitze
sprech' ich den Eid:
Spitze, achte des Spruchs!
Ich weihe deine Wucht,
dass sie ihn werfe;
deine Schärfe segne ich,
das sie ihn schneide:
denn, brach seine Eide er all',
schwur Meineid jetzt dieser Mann!

DIE MANNEN

(im höchsten Aufruhr)

Hilf, Donner!
Tose dein Wetter,
zu schweigen die wütende Schmach!

SIEGFRIED

Gunther, wehr' deinem Weibe,
das schamlos Schande dir lügt!
Gönn't ihr Weil' und Ruh',
der wilden Felsenfrau,
dass ihre freche Wut sich lege,
die eines Unhold's
arge List
wider uns alle erregt!
Ihr Mannen, kehret euch ab!
lasst das Weibergekeif!
Als Zage weichen wir gern,
gilt es mit Zungen den Streit.

(dicht zu Gunther tretend)

Glaub', mehr zürnt es mich als dich,

SIEGFRIED

Are you so careless
of your honor?
The tongue then—that condemns
you—
must I accuse it of lying?
Hear, if I broke my faith!
Blood-brotherhood
was my promise to Gunther,
Needful, my trusty sword,
guarded the solemn oath;
its sharpness stood as barrier
against this wretched bride.

BRÜNNHILDE

You hero in fraud,
look how you lie!
Why do you vainly
swear by your sword!
I know quite well its sharpness,
and also the scabbard,
within which, snugly
slept on the wall,
Needful, that loyal friend,
while his master paid court to his
bride.

THE MEN

(crowding together, angrily)

What, did he turn traitor,
sullying Gunther's honor?

GUNTHER

My shame is heavy,
void of defense,
if you don't answer
what she has said.

GUTRUNE

Faithless, Siegfried?
Are you untrue?
Attest that the tale
she tells is false.

THE MEN

Clear yourself now,
if you are true.
Silence her clamors!
Swear with an oath!

SIEGFRIED

Silence her clamors?
Swear with an oath?
Which of you men here
will lend me his arms?

HAGEN

I have here my spear-point:
that I will lend.
It guards the honor of oaths.

(The men form a ring round Siegfried
and Hagen. The latter extends the
spear. Siegfried lays two fingers of
his right hand upon the point.)

SIEGFRIED

Shining spear!
Hallowed weapon!
Come to the aid of my honor!
By this shining spear-point
Here is my oath:
Spear-point, hark to my words!
If sharpness can pierce me,
yours be the point;
and if death must attack me,
yours be the blow—
if I have wronged this bride,
if I have frauded my friend.

BRÜNNHILDE

(enters the circle wrathfully, thrusts
Siegfried's hand from the spear and
touches the point with her own)

Shining spear!
Hallowed weapon!
Come to the aid of my honor!
By this shining spear-point
here is my oath:
spear-point, hark to my words!
I consecrate your weight
to his undoing!
And I bless this keen-edged blade
for his destruction!
He stands here a traitor to vows,
perfidious! Fraud is his name!

THE MEN

(in an uproar)

Help, Donner!
bring on your thunder
to silence this roaring disgrace!

SIEGFRIED

Gunther, look to this woman,
whose shameless words bring you
shame!
Give her time and rest,
this untamed mountain maid,
until that shrewish rage is quiet,
which by some demon's
artful spite
rouses confusion in all!
You vassals, be on your way.
None but women should scold!
We're cowards, what are we else,
using as weapons our tongues!

(advancing to Gunther)

I'm more annoyed than you

dass schlecht ich sie getäuscht:
der Tarnhelm, dünkt mich fast,
hat halb mich nur gehehlt.
Doch Frauengroll
friedet sich bald:
dass ich dir es gewann,
dankt dir gewiss noch das Weib.
(*Er wendet sich wieder zu den Mannen.*)
Munter, ihr Mannen!
Folgt mir zum Mahl!
Froh zur Hochzeit
helfet ihr Frau'n!
Wonnige Lust
lache nun auf:
In Hof und Hain
heiter vor allen
sollt ihr heute mich seh'n.
Wen die Minne freut,
meinem frohen Mute
tu' es der Glückliche gleich!
(*Er schlingt in ausgelassenem Uebermute seinen Arm um Gutrune und zieht sie mit sich in die Halle; die Mannen und Frauen folgen ihm nach.*
Brünnhilde, Gunther und Hagen bleiben zurück. Gunther hat sich, in tiefer Scham und furchtbarer Verstimmung, mit verhülltem Gesicht abseits niedergesetzt. Brünnhilde, im Vordergrund stehend, blickt Siegfried und Gutrune noch eine Zeitlang schmerzlich nach und senkt dann das Haupt.)

BRÜNNHILDE
Welches Unhold's List
liegt hier verhohlen?
Welches Zaubrer's Rat
regte dies auf?
Wo ist nun mein Wissen
gegen dies Wirrsal?
Wo sind meine Runen
gegen dies Rätsel?
Ach Jammer, Jammer!
Weh', ach Wehe!
All mein Wissen
wies ich ihm zu:
In seiner Macht
hält er die Magd;
in seinen Banden
fasst er die Beute,
die, jammernd ob ihrer Schmach,
jauchzend der Reiche verschenkt!
Wer bietet mir nun das Schwert,
mit dem ich die Bande zerschnitt?

HAGEN
(*dicht an sie herantretend*)

Vertraue mir,
betrog'ne Frau!
Wer dich verriet,
das räche ich.

BRÜNNHILDE
An wem?

HAGEN
An Siegfried, der dich betrog.

BRÜNNHILDE
An Siegfried? du?
(*Sie lacht bitter.*)
Ein einz'ger Blick
seines blitzenden Auges,
das selbst durch die Lügengestalt
leuchtend strahlte zu mir,
deinen besten Mut
machte er bangen!

HAGEN
Doch meinem Speere
spart ihn sein Meineid?

BRÜNNHILDE
Eid und Meineid—
müssige Acht!
Nach Stärk'rem späh',
deinen Speer zu waffnen,
willst du den Stärksten bestehn!

HAGEN
Wohl kenn' ich Siegfried's
siegende Kraft,
wie schwer im Kampf er zu fällen;
d'rum raune nun du
mir klugen Rat,
wie doch der Recke mir wich?

BRÜNNHILDE
O Undank; schändlichster Lohn!
Nicht eine Kunst
war mir bekannt,
die zum Heil nicht half seinem Leib'!
Unwissend zähmt' ihn
mein Zauberspiel,
das ihn vor Wunden nun gewahrt.

HAGEN
So kann keine Wehr ihm schaden?

BRÜNNHILDE
Im Kampfe nicht: doch—
träf'st du im Rücken ihn.
Niemals—das wusst' ich—
wich er dem Feind,
nie reicht er fliehend ihm den Rücken:
an ihm drum spart' ich den Segen.

HAGEN
Und dort trifft ihn mein Speer!
(*Er wendet sich rasch zu Gunther um.*)
Auf, Gunther!
edler Gibichung!
Hier steht dein starkes Weib:
was hängst du dort in Harm?

I played my part so ill.
The Tarnhelm, I suspect,
was but a half disguise.
Yet woman's wrath
quickly abates:
she will then rejoice,
thankful I won her for you.

(*turning again to the men*)

Frolic, good fellows,
come to the feast!
To the wedding, maidens,
make merry!
Joy as you please,
laugh as you will.
In court and grove,
first in the frolic,
watch me revel it up!
You who live and love,
let my jolly spirits
move you to join in my mirth!

(*Zestfully he puts his arms around
Gutrune and draws her into the hall
with him. The men and women follow. Brünnhilde, Gunther and Hagen
remain behind. Gunther, in deep
shame and dejection, with face cov-
ered, has seated himself on one side.
Brünnhilde gazes for a time sorrowfully after Siegfried and Gutrune,
then drops her head.*)

BRÜNNHILDE

Does some devil's plot
lie here in hiding?
Has a wizard's will
brought on this woe?
Where is now my wisdom
'gainst this confusion?
And where are the runes
I need for this riddle?
Ah, sorrow, sorrow!
Woe! Ah, woe!
I gave all my
wisdom to him!
He holds the maid
fast in his power.
I am in bondage,
held as his booty,
whom, weeping—though in despite—
lightly the hero casts off!
Who'll offer me now the sword
with which I may sever my bonds?

HAGEN (*approaching*)

Just trust in me,
offended wife!
I'll right your wrongs
and wreak revenge!

BRÜNNHILDE

On whom?

HAGEN

On Siegfried, treacherous cheat!

BRÜNNHILDE

On Siegfried? You?

(*She laughs bitterly.*)

One single glance
of his eyes as they lighten—
which even disguises could not hide,
when they dazzled my sight—
would lay low
your most valorous spirits!

HAGEN

Why should his falsehood
spare him from vengeance?

BRÜNNHILDE

Truth, and falsehood—
wearisome words!
Seek stronger means
to enforce your weapon,
if you would slay the most strong!

HAGEN

I know his conquering
power quite well.
It's hard to vanquish this hero.
So whisper to me
a cunning spell
to make this warrior weak.

BRÜNNHILDE

O thankless! Shameful return!
All of the arts
within my lore
were employed to guard Siegfried's
life.
Yet he knows not
of my magic spells
that keep him free from every wound.

HAGEN

You mean there's no blade can hurt
him?

BRÜNNHILDE

In battle, no—yet—
if you can strike his back . . .
Never—I know this—
would he retreat.
He never showed his back to foemen.
So there I spared my protection.

HAGEN

My spear knows where to strike.

(*He turns to Gunther.*)

Up, Gunther! .
Noble Gibichung!
Here stands your valiant wife.
Why hang around and mope?

GUNTHER
(*leidenschaftlich auffahrend*)
O Schmach!
O Schande!
Wehe mir,
dem jammervollsten Manne!

HAGEN
In Schande liegst du—
leugn' ich das?

BRÜNNHILDE
O feiger Mann!
falscher Genoss!
Hinter dem Helden
hehltest du dich,
dass Preise des Ruhmes
er dir erränge!
Tief wohl sank
das teure Geschlecht,
das solche Zagen gezeugt!

GUNTHER (*ausser sich*)
Betrüger ich—und betrogen!
Verräter ich—und verraten!
Zermalmt mir das Mark!
Zerbrecht mir die Brust!
Hilf, Hagen!
Hilf meiner Ehre!
Hilf deiner Mutter,
die mich—auch ja gebar!

HAGEN
Dir hilft kein Hirn,
dir hilft keine Hand:
dir hilft nur—Siegfried's Tod!

GUNTHER
Siegfried's Tod!

HAGEN
Nur der sühnt deine Schmach.

GUNTHER
(*von Grausen gepackt, vor sich hinstarrend*)
Blutbrüderschaft
schwuren wir uns!

HAGEN
Des Bundes Bruch
sühne nun Blut!

GUNTHER
Brach er den Bund?

HAGEN
Da er dich verriet.

GUNTHER
Verriet er mich?

BRÜNNHILDE
Dich verriet er,
und mich verrietet ihr Alle!
Wär ich gerecht,
alles Blut der Welt
büsste mir nicht eure Schuld!
Doch des Einen Tod
taugt mir für Alle:

Siegfried falle—
zur Sühne für sich und euch!

HAGEN
(*nahe zu Gunther gewendet*)
Er falle—dir zum Heil!
Ungeheure Macht wird dir,
gewinnst von ihm du den Ring,
den der Tod ihm wohl nur entreisst.

GUNTHER
Brünnhilde's Ring?

HAGEN (*leise*)
Des Niblungen Reif.

GUNTHER
(*schwer seufzend*)
So wär' es Siegfried's Ende!

HAGEN
Uns allen frommt sein Tod.

GUNTHER
Doch, Gutrune, ach!
der ich ihn gönnte:
Straften den Gatten wir so,
wie bestünden wir vor ihr?

BRÜNNHILDE (*wild auffahrend*)
Was riet mir mein Wissen?
Was wiesen mich Runen?
Im hilflosen Elend
ahnet mir's hell:
Gutrune heisst der Zauber,
der den Gatten mir entrückt!
Angst treffe sie!

HAGEN (*zu Gunther*)
Muss sein Tod sie betrüben,
verhehlt sei ihr die Tat.
Auf munt'res Jagen
ziehen wir morgen:
der Edle braust uns voran—
ein Eber bracht' ihn da um.

GUNTHER UND BRÜNNHILDE
So soll es sein!
Siefried falle!
Sühn' er die Schmach,
die er mir schuf!
Eidtreue
hat er getrogen:
mit seinem Blute
büss' er die Schuld!
Allrauner!
Rächender Gott!
Schwurwissender
Eideshort!
Wotan! Wotan!
Wende dich her!
Weise die schrecklich
heilige Schar,
hieher zu horchen
dem Racheschwur!

GUNTHER (*rising sorrowfully*)
O shame!
Dishonor!
Woe is me,
most sorrowful of mortals!

HAGEN
Your shame is mighty,
who can doubt?

BRÜNNHILDE
O craven man!
Treacherous mate!
Hiding behind
the hero you crouched,
awaiting the prize
from him who was victor!
Low indeed
our race must have sunk
to bear a dastard like you!

GUNTHER (*beside himself*)
Deceived I—and deceived one!
Betrayer I—and betrayed one!
I'm crushed to the core,
and pierced to the heart!
Help, Hagen!
Help save my honor!
Help for your mother!
For you, too, are her son!

HAGEN
No brain can help,
no hand can give aid.
Your help is—Siegfried's death!

GUNTHER
Siegfried's death!

HAGEN
Just this wipes out your shame!

GUNTHER (*staring horror-struck*)
Blood-brotherhood
made us as one!

HAGEN
The broken bond
calls for his blood!

GUNTHER
Did he break faith?

HAGEN
In betraying you!

GUNTHER
Was he untrue?

BRÜNNHILDE
He betrayed you,
and all have wrought my betrayal!
Were I avenged,
all the blood on earth
would not suffice for your crime!
Yet the death of one
fulfills all justice:
Siegfried's downfall
pays sins of his own—and yours!

HAGEN (*turning to Gunther*)
His downfall—brings you gain.
Power unheard of will be yours
if you can win but the ring,
which his death alone can achieve.

GUNTHER (*softly*)
Brünnhilde's ring?

HAGEN
The Nibelungen ring.

GUNTHER
(*sighing deeply*)
Must this be Siegfried's downfall?

HAGEN
His death will help us all.

GUNTHER
But, Gutrune, ah,
to whom I gave him!
If we destroyed her husband
could we stand before her face?

BRÜNNHILDE (*furiously*)
What good was my wisdom?
What use was my cunning?
My helpless despair
makes all things now clear!
Gutrune is the magic
that bewitched my lord away!
Woe strike her down!

HAGEN (*to Gunther*)
Since his death may afflict her,
we must conceal the truth.
We'll go a-hunting
early tomorrow.
Our man will rush on ahead—
we'll find him gored by a boar.

GUNTHER, BRÜNNHILDE
So shall it be!
Doomed is Siegfried!
Let him now pay
dear for my shame!
He played false
with vows that he swore to:
so let his blood
pay for his guilt!
All-knowing
god of revenge!
All-witnessing
lord of vows!
Wotan! Wotan!
Come to our aid!
Bring on your holy,
terrible troops
hither to hearken
to vengeful vows!

HAGEN

So soll es sein!
Siegfried falle:
Sterb' er dahin,
der strahlende Held!
Mein ist der Hort,
mir muss er gehören:
Drum sei der Reif
ihm entrissen.
Albenvater,
gefallener Fürst!
Nachthüter!
Niblungenherr!
Alberich! Alberich!
Achte auf mich!
Weise von neuem
der Niblungen Schar,
dir zu gehorchen,
des Ringes Herrn!

(*Gunther und Brünnhilde wenden sich
heftig zur Halle. Siegfried und Gutrune—Siegfried mit einem Eichen-
kranz, Gutrune bunte Blumen auf
dem Haupte — treten ihnen, zur
Nachfolge auffordernd, am Eingange
entgegen. Gunther fasst Brünnhilde
bei der Hand, und folgt mit ihr
schnell. Hagen bleibt allein zurück.*)

DRITTER AUFZUG

Wildes Wald- und Felsental

*Am Rheine, welcher im Hintergrunde
an einem steilen Abhange vorbei-
fliesst. Die drei Rheintöchter tauchen
aus der Flut auf, und schwimmen
während des folgenden Gesanges in
einem Kreise umher.*

DIE DREI RHEINTÖCHTER

Frau Sonne
sendet lichte Strahlen;
Nacht liegt in der Tiefe:
Einst war sie hell,
da heil und hehr
des Vaters Gold noch in ihr glänzte!
Rheingold!
Klares Gold!
wie hell du einstens strahltest,
hehrer Stern der Tiefe!
Weialala, weialala
heia, leia, wallalala
heialala, leilalala.

Frau Sonne,
sende uns den Helden,
der das Gold uns wieder gäbe!
Liess' er es uns,
dein lichtes Auge
neideten dann wir nicht länger!
Rheingold!
Klares Gold!
Wie froh du dann strahltest
freier Stern der Tiefe!
(*Man hört Siegfried's Horn von der
Höhe her.*)

WOGLINDE

Ich höre sein Horn.

WELLGUNDE

Der Helde naht.

FLOSSHILDE

Lasst uns beraten!
(*Sie tauchen schnell in die Flut, Siegfried erscheint auf dem Abhange in
vollen Waffen.*)

SIEGFRIED

Ein Albe führte mich irr',
Dass ich die Fährte verlor:
He Schelm! in welchem Berge
bargst du so schnell mir das Wild?

DIE DREI RHEINTÖCHTER
(*wieder auftauchend*)

Siegfried!

FLOSSHILDE

Was schiltst du so in den Grund?

WELLGUNDE

Welchem Alben bist du gram?

WOGLINDE

Hat dich ein Nicker geneckt?

ALLE DREI

Sag' es, Siegfried, sag' es uns!

SIEGFRIED
(*sie lächelnd betrachtend*)

Entzücktet ihr zu euch
den zottigen Gesellen,
der mir verschwand?
Ist's euer Friedel,
euch lustigen Frauen
lass' ich ihn gern.
(*Die Mädchen lachen laut auf.*)

WOGLINDE

Siegfried, was gibst du uns,
wenn wir das Wild dir gönnen?

SIEGFRIED

Noch bin ich beutelos:
so bittet, was ihr begehrt!

HAGEN

So shall it be!
Doomed is Siegfried!
Thus let him die,
Thus let him die,
that radiant heart!
Mine is the hoard,
I rightfully own it.
So let it be
taken from him!
Elfin-father!
You fallen prince!
Night-guardian!
Nibelung's lord!
Alberich! Alberich!
Come to my aid!
Summon the Nibelungs
and warn them anew
you are their leader,
the ring's true lord!

(*As Gunther and Brünnhilde turn toward the hall they are met by the outcoming bridal procession. Siegfried, wearing a wreath of oak leaves, and Gutrune, crowned with flowers, meet them at the entrance. Gunther grasps Brünnhilde by the hand and follows with her. Hagen alone remains behind.*)

ACT THREE

A Wild, Woody and Rocky Valley

The Rhine flows past the back by a steep cliff. The three Rhine-daughters, Voglinda, Vellgunda and Flosshilda, rise to the surface of the water and swim around as if in a dance, as they sing the following song.

THE THREE RHINE-MAIDENS

O sun-god,
send your rays of glory.
Night lies on the waters.
Once they were bright,
when, fair and clear,
our father's gold
lit up their darkness.
Rhinegold!
Gleaming gold!
How bright was once your radiance,
noble star of waters!
Weialala, weialala,
leia, leia, walalala,
leila la la, leila la la.
O sun-god,

send to us the hero
who will give us back our treasure.
If it were ours,
we nevermore
would envy your eye for its radiance.
Rhinegold!
Gleaming gold!
How glad was your radiance,
noble star of waters!
(*Siegfried's horn is heard from the heights.*)

VOGLINDA

The sound of his horn!

VELLGUNDA

The hero comes.

FLOSSHILDA

Let us take counsel.
(*They all dive down quickly. Siegfried appears on the cliff in full armor.*)

SIEGFRIED

An elfin led me astray,
and so I'm lost on my way.
Hey, rogue! What mountain land
has served for concealing my game?

RHINE-MAIDENS
(*rising again*)
Siegfried!

FLOSSHILDA

But why scold so at the ground?

VELLGUNDA

Who's the elfin that you blame?

VOGLINDA

Is it a nixie that nicks?

ALL THREE

Tell us, Siegfried, speak to us!

SIEGFRIED
(*smilingly*)
Did you entice that shaggy
comrade who has
got away from my hands?
If he's your sweetheart,
you're welcome to keep him,
frolicsome maids.
(*They laugh aloud.*)

VOGLINDA

Siegfried, what will you give,
if we return your quarry?

SIEGFRIED

Still am I bootyless,
but tell me what you desire.

WELLGUNDE
Ein gold'ner Ring
glänzt dir am Finger—
DIE DREI RHEINTÖCHTER
Den gib uns!
SIEGFRIED
Einen Riesenwurm
erschlug ich um den Reif,
für eines schlechten Bären Tatzen
böt' ich ihn nun zum Tausch?
WOGLINDE
Bist du so karg?
WELLGUNDE
So geizig beim Kauf?
FLOSSHILDE
Freigebig
solltest Frauen du sein.
SIEGFRIED
Verzehrt' ich an euch mein Gut,
dess' zürnte mir wohl mein Weib.
FLOSSHILDE
Sie ist wohl schlimm?
WELLGUNDE
Sie schlägt dich wohl?
WOGLINDE
Ihre Hand fühlt schon der Held!
(Sie lachen.)
SIEGFRIED
Nun lacht nur lustig zu!
In Harm lass' ich euch doch:
denn giert ihr nach dem Ring,
euch Nickern geb' ich ihn nie.
FLOSSHILDE
So schön!
WELLGUNDE
So stark!
WOGLINDE
So gehrenswert!
DIE DREI RHEINTÖCHTER
Wie schade, dass er geizig ist!
(Sie lachen und tauchen unter. Sieg-
fried steigt tiefer in den Grund
hinab.)
SIEGFRIED
Was leid' ich doch
das karge Lob?
Lass' ich so mich schmäh'n?
Kämen sie wieder,
zum Wasserrand,
den Ring könnten sie haben.
He, he! ihr munt'ren
Wasserminnen!
Kommt rasch: ich schenk' euch den
Ring!
(Er hat den Ring vom Finger gezogen
und hält ihn in die Höhe. Die Rhein-
töchter tauchen wieder auf und zei-
gen sich ernst und feierlich.)

DIE DREI RHEINTÖCHTER
Behalt' ihn, Held,
und wahr ihn wohl,
bis du das Unheil errätst,
das in dem Ring du hegst.
Froh fühlst du dich dann,
befrei'n wir dich von dem Fluch.

SIEGFRIED
(gelassen den Ring wieder ansteckend)
So singet, was ihr wisst!

DIE RHEINTÖCHTER
Siegfried! Siegfried! Siegfried!
Schlimmes wissen wir dir.
Zu deinem Unheil
wahrst du den Ring!
Aus des Rheines Gold
ist der Reif geglüht:
Der ihn listig geschmiedet
und schmählich verlor,
der verfluchte ihn,
in fernster Zeit,
zu zeugen den Tod
dem, der ihn trüg'.
Wie den Wurm du fälltest,
so fällst auch du,
und heute noch
—so heissen wir's dir
tauschest den Ring du uns nicht,
im tiefen Rhein ihn zu bergen.
Nur seine Flut
sühnet den Fluch!

SIEGFRIED
Ihr listigen Frauen,
lass't das sein!
Traut' ich kaum eurem Schmeicheln,
euer Drohen trügt mich noch minder!

DIE RHEINTÖCHTER
Siegfried! Siegfried!
Wir weisen dich wahr:
Weiche! weiche dem Fluch!
Ihn flochten nächtlich
webende Nornen
in des Urgesetzes Seil.

SIEGFRIED
Mein Schwert zerschwang einen Speer:
des Urgesetzes
ewiges Seil,
flochten sie wilde
Flüche hinein,
Notung zerhaut es den Nornen!
Wohl warnte mich einst

VELLGUNDA
A golden ring
juts on your finger—

ALL THREE MAIDENS
We'd like it!

SIEGFRIED
But to win that ring
I slew a dragon foe.
Why should I let you have it
for the paws of a measly bear?

VOGLINDA
Stingy indeed!

VELLGUNDA
So higgling in deals!

FLOSSHILDA
Free-givers
please the women the best.

SIEGFRIED
My wife would become quite mad
if I were to waste my goods.

FLOSSHILDA
Is she that strict?

VELLGUNDA
She beats you then?

VOGLINDA
He has often felt her hand!
(They laugh.)

SIEGFRIED
Enjoy your merry laugh!
I still leave you in grief:
don't hope for your desire,
I'll never give you the ring!

FLOSSHILDA
So fair!

VELLGUNDA
So strong!

VOGLINDA
So meet for love!

ALL THREE MAIDENS
What pity he's a stingy man!
(They laugh and dive down. Sieg-
    fried descends nearer the ground.)

SIEGFRIED
Why should I bear
this mean report?
Must I thus be shamed?
If they would come
near the shore again,
the fair nixies could have it.
Hey, hey, you merry
water-beauties!
Come quick! I'll give you the ring!
(He takes it from his hands and holds
    it up. The Rhine-maidens dive up
    again, now solemn and grave.)

ALL THREE MAIDENS
Hold on to it
and guard it well,
until the bad luck is known
that lives within the ring.
Then you will be glad
if we cancel its curse.

SIEGFRIED
(quietly putting the ring on his finger
    again)
Then sing me what you know.

THE RHINE-MAIDENS
Siegfried! Siegfried! Siegfried!
Sorrow lies in your way!
Let go the ring
or else you are doomed.
It was made of gold
from the river Rhine.
He who cunningly forged it,
and lost it in shame,
put a curse on it,
to farthest time,
to bring to his death
each of its lords.
As you slew the dragon
you shall be slain,
and on this day—
we tell you this now —
if you deny us the ring
which we would hide in the Rhine-
    deeps.
Only the waves
cancel the curse!

SIEGFRIED
You women of cunning,
let it be!
I'm not moved by your flattery,
and alarms are still less disturbing!

THE RHINE-MAIDENS
Siegfried! Siegfried!
We tell you the truth!
Yield it! Turn from the curse!
It makes a strand
once set by the weavers
in the cord
of primal law.

SIEGFRIED
My sword once shattered a spear.
And if the Norns
have woven this strand,
putting a curse
in destiny's cord,
Needful shall sunder the weaving.
The dragon once warned me

vor dem Fluch ein Wurm,
doch das Fürchten lehrt' er mich nicht!
Der Welt Erbe
gewänne mir ein Ring:
für der Minne Gunst
miss' ich ihn gern.
Ich geb' ihn euch, gönnt ihr mir Lust.
Doch bedroh't ihr mir Leben und Leib:
fasste er nicht
eines Finger's Wert,
den Reif entringt ihr mir nicht!
Denn Leben und Leib
seht!—so
werf' ich sie weit von mir!
(*Er hat eine Erdscholle vom Boden
aufgehoben und mit den letzten
Worten sie über sein Haupt hinter
sich geworfen.*)

DIE RHEINTÖCHTER

Kommt, Schwestern!
Schwindet dem Toren!
So weise und stark
verwähnt sich der Held
als gebunden und blind er doch ist.
Eide schwur er—
und achtet sie nicht!
Runen weiss er—
und rät sie nicht!
Ein hehrstes Gut
ward ihm gegönnt—
dass er's verworfen
weiss er nicht:
nur den Ring, der zum Tod ihm taugt,
den Reif nur will er sich wahren!
Leb' wohl, Siegfried!
Ein stolzes Weib
wird noch heut' dich Argen beerben:
Sie beut uns bess'res Gehör.
Zu ihr! Zu ihr! Zu ihr!
(*Sie schwimmen singend davon. Siegfried sieht ihnen lächelnd nach.*)

SIEGFRIED

Im Wasser wie am Lande
lernte nun ich Weiberart:
Wer nicht ihrem Schmeicheln traut,
den schrecken sie mit Drohen;
wer dem nun kühnlich trotzt,
dem kommt dann ihr Keifen dran!
Und doch—
trüg' ich nicht Gutrun' Treu'
der zieren Frauen eine
hätt' ich mir frisch gezähmt!
(*Jagdhornrufe kommen von der Höhe
näher: Siegfried antwortet lustig auf
seinem Horne. Gunther, Hagen und
Mannen kommen während des Folgenden von der Höhe herab.*)

HAGEN
(*noch auf der Höhe*)

Hoiho!

SIEGFRIED

Hoiho!

DIE MANNEN

Hoiho! hoiho!

HAGEN

Finden wir endlich,
wohin du flog'st?

SIEGFRIED

Kommt herab! Hier ist's frisch und
kühl.
(*Die Mannen sind nun alle auf der
Höhe und steigen mit Hagen und
Gunther herab.*)

HAGEN

Hier rasten wir
und rüsten das Mahl.
Lasst ruh'n die Beute
und bietet die Schläuche!
(*Jagdbeute wird zu Hauf gelegt; Trink-
hörner und Schläuche werden her-
vorgeholt. Dann lagert sich alles.*)
Der uns das Wild verscheuchte
nun sollt' ihr Wunder hören
was Siegfried sich erjagt.

SIEGFRIED
(*lachend*)

Schlimm steht es um mein Mahl:
Von eurer Beute
bitte ich für mich.

HAGEN

Du beutelos?

SIEGFRIED

Auf Waldjagd zog ich aus,
doch Wasserwild zeigte sich nur:
War ich dazu recht beraten,
drei wilde Wasservögel
hätt' ich euch wohl gefangen,
die dort auf dem Rhein mir sangen,
erschlagen würd' ich noch heut'.
(*Gunther erschrickt und blickt düster
auf Hagen.*)

HAGEN

Das wäre üble Jagd,
wenn den Beutelosen selbst
ein lauernd Wild erlegte!

SIEGFRIED

Mich dürstet!
(*Er hat sich zwischen Hagen und Gunther gelagert.*)

of this same curse,
yet he never taught me to fear!
The ring granted me
lordship of the earth,
yet the grace of love
buys it from me.
You'd have it too,
just for your love.
But your threat to my life and my
    limbs
means not as much
as a finger's worth.
You'll never gain the ring thus.
My life and my limbs—see—
so—that's what I think of them!

(*Here he picks up a clod of earth,
    holds it aloft, and at these words
    throws it behind him.*)

THE RHINE-MAIDENS

Come, sisters,
Fly from this numbskull!
He fancies himself
so strong and so wise,
but he's fettered and utterly blind!
He has sworn oaths,
and heeded them not!
Runes were given,
he used them not!
A worthy good
was once his prize:
he cast it from him
unawares.
But the ring, which will bring him
    death,
the ring he wants to hold on to!
Farewell, Siegfried!
A noble wife will today
inherit your token,
She'll listen better than you.
To her! To her! To her!

(*They swim away singing. Siegfried
    looks after them, smiling.*)

SIEGFRIED

In water, as on the land,
I've learned a lot of woman's wiles:
When all their cajolings fail
they bear one down with threatenings;
and if these fail to work
they lash him with scolding words!
And yet—
were I not Gutrune's spouse,
a girl as fair as these
would suit me well—once she's tamed!

(*Horns are heard approaching. Sieg-
    fried answers gaily on his own horn.
    Gunther, Hagen and the men come
    down the hills during the following.*)

HAGEN

(*His voice is still in the distance.*)
Hoiho!

SIEGFRIED

Hoiho!

THE MEN

Hoiho! Hoiho!

HAGEN

Finally we find you!
Where were you hidden?

SIEGFRIED

Come on down!
Here it's fresh and cool!

(*The men appear on the cliff and fol-
    low down after Hagen and Gunther.*)

HAGEN

We'll rest right here,
and fix up the meal!
Set down the booty
and offer the wineskins.

(*They lay the game in a heap. Wine-
    skins and drinking horns are pro-
    duced. All lie down.*)

You scared away the quarry,
but let us hear of wonders
that Siegfried's gained in hunt!

SIEGFRIED (*laughing*)

Bad—nothing I can eat!
I must depend on you
if I'm to dine.

HAGEN

No game at all?

SIEGFRIED

I went on through the woods,
but only found waterfowl there:
had I only reckoned rightly,
I would have captured three
fair birds there in the water,
who sang from the Rhine a warning
that I should die today.

(*Gunther starts, and looks gloomily at
    at Hagen.*)

HAGEN

A grievous, fearful hunt,
if a lurking beast should slay
the empty-handed hunter!

SIEGFRIED

I'm thirsty!

(*He has seated himself between Hagen
    and Gunther.*)

HAGEN

(*indem er für Siegfried ein Trinkhorn füllen lässt und es diesem dann darreicht*)

Ich hörte sagen, Siegfried,
der Vögel Sangessprache
verstündest du wohl:
So wäre das wahr?

SIEGFRIED

Seit lange acht' ich
des Lallens nicht mehr.
(*Er trinkt und reicht dann sein Horn Gunther.*)
Trink', Gunther, trink'!
Dein Bruder bringt es dir.

GUNTHER

(*gedankenvoll und schwermütig in das Horn blickend*)

Du mischtest matt und bleich:
dein Blut allein darin!

SIEGFRIED (*lachend*)

So misch' es mit dem deinen!
(*Er giesst aus Gunther's Horn in das seine, so dass es überläuft.*)
Nun floss gemischt es über:
Der Mutter Erde
lass' das ein Labsal sein!

GUNTHER (*seufzend*)

Du überfroher Held!

SIEGFRIED

(*leise zu Hagen*)

Ihm macht Brünnhilde Müh'?

HAGEN

Verstünd' er sie so gut,
wie du der Vögel Sang!

SIEGFRIED

Seit Frauen ich singen hörte,
vergass ich der Vöglein ganz.

HAGEN

Doch einst vernahmst du sie?

SIEGFRIED

Heil! Gunther!
Grämlicher Mann!
Dank'st du es mir,
so sing' ich dir Mären
aus meinen jungen Tagen.

GUNTHER

Die hör' ich gern.
(*Alle lagern sich nahe um Siegfried, welcher allein aufrecht sitzt, während die anderen tiefer gestreckt liegen.*)

HAGEN

So singe, Held!

SIEGFRIED

Mime hiess
ein mürrischer Zwerg;
in des Neides Zwang
zog er mich auf,
dass einst das Kind,
wann kühn es erwuchs,
einen Wurm ihm fällt' im Wald,
der faul dort hütet' einen Hort.
Er lehrte mich schmieden
und Erze schmelzen:
doch was der Künstler
selber nicht konnt',
des Lehrling's Mute
musst' es gelingen—
eines zerschlag'nen Stahles Stücke
neu zu schweissen zum Schwert.
Des Vater's Wehr
fügt' ich mir neu;
nagelfest
schuf ich mir Notung.
Tüchtig zum Kampf
dünkt' er dem Zwerg:
der führte mich nun zum Wald;
dort fällt' ich Fafner, den Wurm.
Jetzt aber merkt
wohl auf die Mär':
Wunder muss ich euch melden.
Von des Wurmes Blut
mir brannten die Finger;
sie führt' ich kühlend zum Mund:
Kaum netzt' ein wenig
die Zunge das Nass.
Was da die Vöglein sangen
das konnt' ich flugs versteh'n:
Auf Aesten sass es und sang—
"Hei, Siegfried gehört nun
der Niblungen Hort!
Oh! fänd' in der Höhle
den Hort er jetzt!
Wollt' er den Tarnhelm gewinnen,
der taugt' ihm zu wonniger Tat:
doch möcht' er den Ring sich erraten
der macht' ihn zum Walter der Welt!"

HAGEN

Ring und Tarnhelm
trugst du nun fort?

DIE MANNEN

Das Vöglein hörtest du wieder?

SIEGFRIED

Ring und Helm
hatt' ich gerafft;
da lauscht' ich wieder
dem wonnigen Laller;
der sass im Wipfel und sang:
"Hei, Siegfried gehört nun

HAGEN

(*filling a drinking-horn and handing it to him*)
I've heard it told me, Siegfried,
you understand the meanings
of birds when they sing.
But can this be so?

SIEGFRIED

It's ages now
since I heeded their chirps.
(*He drinks and hands the horn to Gunther.*)
Drink, Gunther, drink!
Your brother brings the cup!

GUNTHER

(*gazing into the horn with horror*)
The wine is thin and pale:
your blood alone is here!

SIEGFRIED (*laughing*)

Then mingle *your* blood with it.
(*He pours from Gunther's horn into his own, so that it runs over.*)
The cup is overflowing.
Why, here's an offering
outpoured to Mother Earth!

GUNTHER (*sighing*)

You overcheerful man!

SIEGFRIED

(*softly to Hagen*)
Perhaps Brünnhilde has frowned?

HAGEN

He cannot read her mind
the way you do with birds.

SIEGFRIED

Since hearing the songs of women
my mind has forgot the birds.

HAGEN

Yet once you knew them well?

SIEGFRIED

Hey! Gunther!
Gloomy-faced man!
If I am thanked,
I'll sing you some tales
of the time I was a youngster.

GUNTHER

I'll listen well.
(*All gather near Siegfried, who alone sits upright, while the others recline.*)

HAGEN

Well, hero; sing.

SIEGFRIED

Mime was
a surly, old dwarf,
who, enforced by need,
brought me up well,
just so this child
when manly enough
could destroy a dragon foe
who long had brooded on a hoard.
He taught me my smithing,
and metal smelting;
but what this craftsman
could not perform,
apprentice zeal
achieved through daring—
forging from steel some broken pieces,
thus remaking a sword.
My father's blade,
fit for the fight,
gleamed in strength.
Needful, I named it.
Now I could fight,
Mime declared,
and led me straight to the wood.
I slew the dragon that day.
Hark, and attend
well to my tale.
How you will hear a wonder:
when some dragon's blood
splashed on to my finger
I brought the burn to my mouth.
I'd hardly moistened the place with my tongue
when straight the birds were singing
with words that I could hear!
On a branch he sat there and sang:
"Hey, Siegfried now owns
the Nibelung hoard:
Oh, let him but find it
within the cave!
Let him but master the Tarnhelm,
'twill serve him for glorious deeds;
but if he could master the ring,
it would make him the lord of the world!"

HAGEN

Did you bear off
helmet and ring?

THE MEN

What further came from the birdling?

SIEGFRIED

Yes, I took
both helmet and ring,
then harked again
to the wonderful warbler,
who sat above me and sang:
"Hey, Siegfried now owns

der Helm und der Ring.
Oh, traute er Mime,
dem treulosen, nicht!
Ihm sollt' er den Hort nur erheben;
nun lauert er listig am Weg:
nach dem Leben trachtet er Siegfried—
oh, traute Siegfried nicht Mime!"

HAGEN
Es mahnte dich gut?

DIE MANNEN
Vergaltest du Mime?

SIEGFRIED
Mit tödlichem Tranke
trat er zu mir;
bang und stotternd
gestand er mir Böses:
Notung streckte den Strolch.

HAGEN
(lachend)
Was nicht er geschmiedet,
schmeckte doch Mime!
(Er lässt ein Trinkhorn neu füllen und
träufelt den Saft eines Krautes hinein.)
DIE MANNEN
Was wies das Vöglein dich wieder?

HAGEN
(Er reicht Siegfried das Horn. Dieser
blickt gedankenvoll in das Horn und
trinkt dann langsam.)
Trink' erst, Held,
aus meinem Horn:
Ich würzte dir holden Trank,
die Erinnerung hell dir zu wecken,
dass Fernes nicht dir entfalle!

SIEGFRIED
In Leid zu dem Wipfel
lauscht' ich hinauf;
da sass es noch und sang:
"Hei, Siegfried erschlug nun
den schlimmen Zwerg!
Jetzt wüsst' ich ihm noch
das herrlichste Weib.
Auf hohem Felsen sie schläft,
Feuer umbrennt ihren Saal:
durchschritt' er die Brunst,
weckt' er die Braut,
Brünnhilde wäre dann sein!"
(Gunther hört mit wachsendem Erstau-
nen zu.)

HAGEN
Und folgtest du des Vögleins Rat?
SIEGFRIED
Rasch ohne Zögern zog ich nun aus,
bis den feurigen Fels ich traf;
die Lohe durchschritt ich,
und fand zum Lohn—
schlafend ein wonniges Weib
in lichter Waffen Gewand.
Den Helm löst' ich
der herrlichen Maid;
mein Kuss erweckte sie kühn!
Oh! Wie mich brünstig da umschlang
der schönen Brünnhilde Arm!
GUNTHER
(in höchstem Schrecken aufspringend)
Was hör ich!
(Zwei Raben fliegen aus einem Busche
auf, kreisen über Siegfried und fliegen
davon.)
HAGEN
Errätst du auch
dieser Raben Geraun'?
(Siegfried fährt heftig auf, und blickt,
Hagen den Rücken wendend, den
Raben nach.)
HAGEN
Rache rieten sie mir!
(Er stösst seinen Speer in Siegfried's
Rücken; Gunther fällt ihm—zu spät
—in den Arm.)
GUNTHER UND DIE MANNEN
Hagen! was tust du?
Hagen! was tatest du?
(Siegfried schwingt mit beiden Händen
seinen Schild hoch empor, Hagen
damit zu zerschmettern: die Kraft
verlässt ihn, der Schild entsinkt seiner
Hand; er selbst stürzt über ihn zu-
sammen.)
HAGEN
(auf den zu Boden Gestreckten
deutend)
Meineid rächt' ich!
(Er wendet sich ruhig zur Seite ab, und
verliert sich dann einsam über die
Höhe, wo man ihn langsam von
dannen schreiten sieht. Gunther
beugt sich schmerzergriffen zu Siegfried's Seite nieder. Die Mannen
umstehen teilnahmvoll den Sterben-
den. Siegfried von zwei Mannen sitz-
end gehalten, schlägt die Augen
glanzvoll auf.)
SIEGFRIED
Brünnhilde!
Heilige Braut!
Wach' auf! öffne dein Auge!

all the Nibelung hoard,
Oh, let him not trust
in the treacherous dwarf!
He wants to get hold of the treasure.
Take care, for he's lying in wait!
He is seeking now how to slay you.
So trust not Mime, O Siegfried!"

HAGEN

How well did he warn?

THE MEN

What happened with Mime?

SIEGFRIED

He stepped up to me
with poisonous drink.
Pale and stammering,
the rogue stood before me.
Needful stretched him out quick!

HAGEN

(laughing)

Unable to forge it,
yet he could taste it!

(He has another drinking-horn filled,
and drops the juice of an herb into
it.)

THE MEN

And had the bird more to tell you?

HAGEN

(offering the horn to Siegfried, who
looks into it thoughtfully and then
drinks slowly)

Drink first, man,
from out my horn:
I brewed you a special drink
which will waken and brighten your
memories,
so none of the past escapes you.

SIEGFRIED

Once more I looked up
and heard the bird,
for still he sat and sang—
"Hey, Siegfried has struck down
the wicked dwarf!
Now soon he may take
a wonderful wife,
who sleeps surrounded by fire,
high up on a mountain of rock.
Who steps through the fire
wakens the bride:
Brünnhilde then may be his!
(Gunther listens with increasing
astonishment.)

HAGEN

And did you take the birdling's counsel?

SIEGFRIED

Off did I go, I never delayed,
till I came to the fiery rock.
I stepped through fires
and found my prize—
sleeping—a heavenly maid.
She shone in armor of war.
I loosened the helmet she wore.
My kiss awakened the maid.
Then how burningly the lovely
Brünnhilde embraced me!

GUNTHER

(springing up in terror)

What is this?
(Two ravens fly out of a bush, circle
above Siegfried, and then fly away
toward the Rhine.)

HAGEN

Perhaps you know
What those ravens have said?
(Siegfried starts up suddenly, and turning his back to Hagen, looks after the
ravens.)

HAGEN

Vengeance—such as they asked!
(With these words Hagen thrusts his
spear into Siegfried's back. Gunther
catches his arm too late.)

GUNTHER, THE MEN

What have you done here?
What have you done?
(Siegfried swings his shield aloft with
both hands in order to throw it on
Hagen; his strength fails him; the
shield falls back, and he himself falls
back upon it.)

HAGEN

(pointing to the prostrate Siegfried)

Paid the perjured!
(He turns cooly away and gradually
disappears over the height, where his
retreating form is for some time visible. The anguished Gunther bends
over Siegfried. The men stand
around the dying man, full of sym-
pathy. Siegfried, supported by two
men in a sitting posture, opens radiant eyes.)

SIEGFRIED

Brünnhilde!
Open your eyes!
Wake up! Heavenly woman!

Wer verschloss dich
wieder in Schlaf?
Wer band dich in Schlummer so bang?
Der Wecker kam;
er küsst dich wach,
und aber der Braut
bricht er die Bande:
Da lacht ihm Brünnhilde's Lust!
Ach, dieses Auge,
ewig nun offen!
ach, dieses Atems
wonniges Wehen!
Süsses Vergehen—
seliges Grauen—
Brünnhild' bietet mir Gruss!

(*Er sinkt zurück und stirbt. Regungs-
lose Trauer der Umstehenden. Die
Nacht ist hereingebrochen. Auf die
stumme Ermahnung Gunthers erheb-
en die Mannen Siegfrieds Leiche und
geleiten sie, in feierlichem Zuge,
über die Felsenhöhe langsam von
dannen. Der Mond bricht durch die
Wolken und beleuchtet immer heller
den, die Berghöhe erreichenden,
Trauerzug. Vom Rheine sind Nebel
aufgestiegen und erfüllen allmählich
die ganze Bühne, auf welcher der
Trauerzug bereits unsichtbar geworden ist. Nach dem Zwischenspiel,
während dessen die Bühne im Nebel
verhüllt bleibt, verteilen sich die
Nebel wieder, bis endlich die Halle
der Gibichungen, wie im ersten Aufzug, immer klarer hervortritt. Gutrune tritt aus ihrem Gemach in die
Halle heraus.*)*

GUTRUNE

War das sein Horn?
(*Sie lauscht.*)
Nein! noch
kehrt er nicht heim.
Schlimme Träume
störten mir den Schlaf!
Wild wieherte sein Ross:
Lachen Brünnhilde's
weckte mich auf.
Wer war das Weib,
das ich zum Ufer schreiten sah?
Ich fürchte Brünnhild'.
Ist sie daheim?
(*Sie lauscht an einer Türe rechts und
ruft dann leise:*)
Brünnhild'! Brünnhild'!
Bist du wach?
(*Sie öffnet schüchtern und blickt
hinein.*)

HAGEN'S STIMME
(*von aussen sich nähernd*)
Hoiho! hoiho!
Wacht auf! wacht auf!
Lichte! Lichte!
Helle Brände!
Jagdbeute
bringen wir heim.
Hoiho! hoiho!
(*Licht und wachsender Feuerschein
von aussen. Hagen tritt in die Halle.*)
Auf! Gutrun'!
Begrüsse Siegfried!
Der starke Held,
er kehret heim.

GUTRUNE
(*in grosser Angst*)
Was geschah, Hagen?
Nicht hört' ich sein Horn!
(*Mannen und Frauen begleiten, mit
Lichtern und Feuerbränden, in grosser Verwirrung den Zug, der mit Siegfried's Leiche Heimkehrenden, unter
denen Gunther.*)

HAGEN
Der bleiche Held,
nicht bläst er es mehr;
nicht stürmt er zur Jagd,
zum Streite nicht mehr,
noch wirbt er um wonnige Frauen!

GUTRUNE
(*mit wachsendem Entsetzen, während
die Mannen die Leiche auf einer
schnell errichteten Erhöhung nieder-
setzen.*)
Was bringen die?

HAGEN
Eines wilden Ebers Beute:
Siegfried: deinen toten Mann!
(*Gutrune schreit auf, und stürzt über
die Leiche hin. Allgemeine Erschüt-
terung und Trauer. Gunther bemüht
sich um die Ohnmächtige.*)

GUNTHER
Gutrune! holde Schwester!
Hebe dein Auge,
schweige mir nicht!

GUTRUNE
(*wieder zu sich kommend*)
Siegfried!—Siegfried erschlagen!
(*Sie stösst Gunther heftig zurück.*)
Fort! treuloser Bruder!
Du Mörder meines Mannes!
Oh, Hilfe! Hilfe!
Wehe! Wehe!
Sie haben Siegfried erschlagen!

Are you bound
and fettered in sleep?
Who sealed you in slumber like this?
The wakener came:
his kiss aroused!
He frees her—his bride!
breaking her fetters!
The radiant Brünnhilde smiles!
See her eyes now,
open forever!
Ah, that most blissful
breath of my dear one!
Sweet is my passing,
glorious this shuddering!
Brünnhilde cries to me—hail!

(*He sinks back and dies. All manifest
grief. Night has fallen. At Gunther's
gesture the vassals raise Siegfried's
body and bear it away slowly in a
solemn procession over the rocky
heights. The moon breaks through
the clouds and lights the procession
with increasing clearness. A mist rises
from the Rhine which gradually fills
the atmosphere, at which the funeral
procession becomes invisible. After a
musical interlude the mist parts again
until the hall of the Gibichungs, as
in Act I, appears distinctly. Gutrune
comes out of her chamber into the
hall.*)

GUTRUNE

Was that his horn?
            (*She listens.*)
No! He's not yet returned.
I was troubled
by some evil dreams.
Wild whinnies
came from his steed.
Brünnhilde's laughter
awaked me from sleep.
I thought I saw
a woman step down to the shore.
I fear this Brünnhilde!
Is she at home?

        (*She listens at the door and calls.*)
Brünnhilde! Brünnhilde!
Are you up?

(*She opens the door trembling and
looks into the inner room.*)

She is not here.
So was it she
I saw go down upon the shore?
Was that his horn?
No! All silent!
If he only were here!

HAGEN'S VOICE
(*from outside*)
Hoiho! Hoiho!
Wake up! Wake up!
Torches! Torches!
Torches! Light your torches!
Good game
is here from the hunt!
Hoiho! Hoiho!

(*Lights and increasing glow of fires outside. Hagen enters the hall.*)

Up! Gutrune,
and greet your Siegfried!
The mighty hero
is coming home!

GUTRUNE
(*terrified*)
What is this, Hagen?
I heard not his horn.

(*Men and women with torches usher
in, in great agitation, the train with
Siegfried's body. Gunther is among
them.*)

HAGEN
Your pallid man
will blow it no more.
He'll nevermore hie
to hunt or the fight,
nor look for the love of the ladies.

GUTRUNE
(*with increasing dread as the men set
down the body on a hastily erected
bier*)
What do they bring?

HAGEN
See, a savage boar has slain him—
Siegfried—see, your man is dead!

(*Gutrune shrieks and falls senseless o..
the body. General terror and grief.
Gunther attends to his fainting sister.*)

GUNTHER
Gutrune, lovely sister,
do not be downcast!
Don't remain mute!

GUTRUNE
(*coming to*)
Siegfried! Siegfried was murdered!
        (*She repels Gunther.*)
Hence, treacherous brother!
You murderer of my husband!
O help me! Help me!
Horror! Horror!
They all have murdered my Siegfried!

GUNTHER
Nicht klage wider mich!
Dort klage wider Hagen:
Er ist der verfluchte Eber,
der diesen Edlen zerfleischt'.

HAGEN
Bist du mir gram darum?

GUNTHER
Angst und Unheil
greife dich immer!

HAGEN
(mit furchtbarem Trotze herantretend)
Ja denn! Ich hab' ihn erschlagen:
Ich—Hagen—
schlug ihn zu Tod'.
Meinem Speer war er gespart,
bei dem er Meineid sprach.
Heiliges Beuterecht
hab' ich mir nun errungen:
d'rum fordr' ich hier diesen Ring.

GUNTHER
Zurück! was mir verfiel,
sollst nimmer du empfah'n.

HAGEN
Ihr Mannen, richtet mein Recht!

GUNTHER
Rührst du an Gutrune's Erbe,
schamloser Albensohn?

HAGEN
(sein Schwert ziehend)
Des Alben Erbe
fordert so sein Sohn!
(Er dringt auf Gunther ein; dieser
wehrt sich; sie fechten. Die Mannen
werfen sich dazwischen. Gunther fällt
von einem Streiche Hagen's tot dar-
nieder. Gutrune schreit auf.)
Her den Ring!
(Er greift nach Siegfried's Hand: diese
hebt sich drohend empor. Allgemein-
es Entsetzen. Vom Hintergrunde her
schreitet Brünnhilde fest und feierlich
dem Vordergrunde zu.)

BRÜNNHILDE
Schweigt eures Jammers
jauchzenden Schwall!
Das ihr alle verrietet,
zur Rache schreitet sein Weib.
(Sie schreitet ruhig weiter vor.)
Kinder hört' ich
greinen nach der Mutter,

da süsse Milch sie verschüttet:
doch nicht erklang mir
würdige Klage,
des hehrsten Helden wert.

GUTRUNE
(vom Boden sich aufrichtend)
Brünnhilde! Neiderboste!
Du brachtest uns diese Not!
Die du die Männer ihm verhetztest,
weh', dass du dem Haus genah't!

BRÜNNHILDE
Armselige, schweig'!
Sein Eheweib warst du nie:
Als Buhlerin
bandest du ihn.
Sein Mannes-Gemahl bin ich,
der ewige Eide er schwur,
eh' Siegfried je dich ersah.

GUTRUNE
(in heftigster Verzweiflung)
Verfluchter Hagen!
Dass du das Gift mir rietest,
das ihr den Gatten entrückt!
Ach, Jammer!
Wie jäh nun weiss ich's
Brünnhilde war die Traute,
die durch den Trank er vergass!
(Sie wendet sich voll Scheu von Sieg-
fried ab, und beugt sich, in Schmerz
aufgelöst, über Gunther's Leiche: so
verbleibt sie regungslos bis an das
Ende. Hagen steht, auf Speer und
Schild gelehnt, in finsteres Sinnen
versunken.)

BRÜNNHILDE
(wendet sich mit feierlicher Erhebung
an die Männer und Frauen)
Starke Scheite
schichtet mir dort
am Rande des Rhein's zu Hauf:
Hoch und hell
lod're die Glut,
die den edlen Leib
des hehrsten Helden verzehrt!
Sein Ross führet daher,
dass mit mir dem Recken es folge:
denn des Helden heiligste
Ehre zu teilen
verlangt mein eigener Leib.
Vollbringt Brünnhilde's Wort!
(Die jüngeren Männer errichten während des Folgenden vor der Halle,
nahe am Rheinufer, einen mächtigen
Scheithaufen. Frauen schmücken ihn
mit Decken, auf die sie Kräuter und
Blumen streuen. Brünnhilde versinkt
von Neuem in die Betrachtung der
Leiche Siegfrieds.)

GUNTHER

Don't put the blame on me,
but put it on to Hagen.
For he is the boar I spoke of,
who gored the hero to death.

HAGEN

So, are you mad at me?

GUNTHER

Wrath and misery
rack you forever!

HAGEN

(stepping forward in strong defiance)
Well then! Yes, I was his slayer.
I, Hagen, dealt him his death!
And my spear avenged, for on it
he swore perjury.
Now, as my sacred prize—
since I have rightly won it—
I lay my claim here to the ring.

GUNTHER

Keep back! You'll never get
what I declare is mine.

HAGEN

You vassals, speak for my rights!

GUNTHER

So you want Gutrune's dowry,
shameless and greedy elf!

HAGEN

(drawing his sword)
The elf will seize it,
for it's his by right!
(He rushes upon Gunther, who defends
himself. They fight. The vassals
throw themselves between the two.
Gunther is struck by Hagen and falls
dead. Gutrune screams.)
Now the ring!
(Hagen seizes at Siegfried's hand,
which raises itself threateningly aloft.
All remain spellbound with horror.
At this moment Brünnhilde enters
solemnly from the back.)

BRÜNNHILDE

Peace with your clamoring
torrent of words!
You are all my betrayers:
I've come here for my revenge.
(She calmly advances.)
You are children
whining to your mother

about the milk you have spilled!
I've heard no words
of fitting lament
for the noblest man that lived.

GUTRUNE

(rising from the floor)
Brünnhilde! Hatred's victim!
You were the bringer of woe
and you aroused the men against him
just when you came into this house.

BRÜNNHILDE

Poor creature, peace!
You never were wife of his,
but only his mistress, no more.
But I was his lawful wife.
He pledged me eternal devotion.
ere he had seen your face!

GUTRUNE

(in indignant despair)
Accursed Hagen!
You urged me give
the treacherous drink
that made Siegfried change!
Ah, sorrow! Sorrow!
I see it all now!
Brünnhilde was his true love
the cup compelled him forget!
(She turns away in shame from Siegfried, and bends fainting over Gunther's body. In this position she
remains until the end. Hagen stands
leaning defiantly on his spear and
shield, sunk in gloomy meditation.)

BRÜNNHILDE

(turning to all)
Let great logs
be brought to the bank
and heaped in a mighty pile.
Let the flames
leap to the sky
and consume the noble corpse
of this first of all men.
And bring Grane, his horse,
that we both may follow our hero,
for I long to share with my body
the holiest honor due to this man.
Fulfill Brünnhilde's word!
(The young men erect, during the following, before the hall, a huge funeral pyre. The women deck it with
herbs and flowers. Brünnhilde is rapt
in contemplation of the body of Siegfried.)

Wie Sonne lauter
strahlt mir sein Licht:
Der Reinste war er,
der mich verriet!
Die Gattin trügend
—treu dem Freunde—
von der eig'nen Trauten
—einzig ihm teuer
schied er sich durch sein Schwert.
Echter als er
schwur keiner Eide;
treuer als er
hielt keiner Verträge:
laut'rer als er
liebte kein and'rer!
Und doch alle Eide,
alle Verträge,
die treueste Liebe—
trog keiner wie er!
Wisst ihr, wie das ward?
(immer feierlicher)
O ihr, der Eide
heilige Hüter!
Lenkt eu'ren Blick
auf mein blühendes Leid:
erschaut eu're ewige Schuld!
Meine Klage hör',
du hehrster Gott!
Durch seine tapferste Tat,
dir so tauglich erwünscht,
weihtest du den, der sie gewirkt,
dem Fluche, dem du verfielest:
mich musste
der Reinste verraten,
dass wissend würde ein Weib!
Weiss ich nun, was dir frommt?
Alles! Alles!
Alles weiss ich:
alles ward mir nun frei!
Auch deine Raben
hör' ich rauschen:
Mit bang' ersehnter Botschaft
send' ich die beiden nun heim.
Ruhe! Ruhe, du Gott!
(Sie winkt den Mannen, Siegfried's Leiche aufzuheben und auf das Scheitgerüste zu tragen; zugleich zieht sie von Siegfried's Finger den Ring und betrachtet ihn während des Folgenden.)
Mein Erbe nun
nehm' ich zu eigen.
Verfluchter Reif!
Furchtbarer Ring!
Dein Gold fass' ich,
und geb' es nun fort.
Der Wassertiefe
weise Schwestern,

des Rheines schwimmende Töchter,
euch dank' ich redlichen Rat!
Was ihr begehrt,
ich geb' es euch:
aus meiner Asche
nehmt es zu eigen!
Das Feuer, das mich verbrennt,
rein'ge vom Fluche den Ring!
Ihr in der Flut
löset ihn auf,
und lauter bewahrt
das lichte Gold,
das euch zum Unheil geraubt.
(Sie wendet sich nach hinten, wo Siegfried's Leiche bereits auf dem Gerüste ausgestreckt liegt, und entreisst einem Manne den mächtigen Feuerbrand.)
Fliegt heim ihr Raben!
Raunt es eurem Herrn,
was hier am Rhein ihr gehört!
An Brünnhilde's Felsen
fahrt vorbei:
der dort noch lodert,
weiset Loge nach Walhall!
Denn der Götter Ende
dämmert nun auf.
So werf' ich den Brand
in Walhall's prangende Burg.
(Sie schleudert den Brand in den Holzstoss, der sich schnell hell entzündet. Zwei Raben sind vom Ufer aufgeflogen, und verschwinden nach dem Hintergrunde zu. Brünnhilde gewahrt ihr Ross, welches soeben zwei Männer hereinführen.)
Grane, mein Ross,
sei mir gegrüsst!
(Sie ist ihm entgegen gesprungen, fasst es und entzäumt es schnell: dann neigt sie sich traulich zu ihm.)
Weisst du auch, mein Freund,
wohin ich dich führe?
Im Feuer leuchtend
liegt dort dein Herr,
Siegfried, mein seliger Held.
Dem Freunde zu folgen
wieherst du freudig?
Lockt dich zu ihm
die lachende Lohe?
Fühl' meine Brust auch,
wie sie entbrennt;
helles Feuer
das Herz mir erfasst,
ihn zu umschlingen,
umschlossen von ihm,
in mächtigster Minne
vermählt ihm zu sein!

He dazzles like the
sun in his strength!
The purest was he,
yet he played false!
Disloyal to Brünnhilde,
yet loyal to friendship,
he set up a weapon,
placed it between us,
barring love from his love
No one was truer,
swearing pledges;
no one was truer
in truth to compacts;
never was man
purer in loving.
Yet in all his pledges,
all of his compacts,
all love and all honor—
none failed as did he!
Know you how that was?

(looking up)

O you, who guard
the honor of pledges!
Look for a while
on my flourishing woe!
Look down on the guilt that is yours!
Hear my sad complaint,
O god most high!
Through Siegfried's highest of deeds,
which you hoped for so much,
doom from your hand
fell on his head,
the curse that must soon strike Wotan.
He—purest
of heroes—betrayed me,
that thus a wife might be wise!
Do I know what you want?
All things! All things!
All are known now!
All is clear to me now!
Hark to your ravens!
Hear their rustling?
With tidings long awaited
let me send both of them home.
Henceforth quiet, O god!

*(She signs to the men to bear Sieg-
fried's body to the funeral pyre, and
draws from his finger the ring, which
she contemplates.)*

The dower comes
back to Brünnhilde.
Accursed round!
Terrible ring!
I now grasp you
and cast you away!
O wise and knowing
water maidens,
you gliding girls of the river,
thank you for sound, frank advice.
What you desire
you now shall have.
From out my ashes
take your possession!
The fire that burns my frame
cleanses the ring of its curse!
You in the Rhine,
wash it away,
and safely preserve
the gleaming gold,
that once was robbed to your bane.

*(She turns to Siegfried's body on the
pyre, and takes a huge firebrand
from a man.)*

Fly home, you ravens!
Whisper to your ruler
the things you heard by the Rhine.
And go by the way of Brünnhilde's
   rock!
The place still blazes.
Send the fire-god
to Valhall,
For the final dusk
has come to all gods!
So—now hurl the brand
at Valhall's glittering pomp.

*(She flings the torch into the pyre,
which quickly kindles brightly. Two
ravens fly up from the rocks by the
shore and disappear. Brünnhilde perceives the horse, led on by two men.)*

Grane, my horse!
We meet once more!

*(She springs toward him, and unbridles
him, then bends affectionately to
him.)*

Do you know, my friend,
just where we are faring?
In radiant fires
there lies your lord,
Siegfried, the lord of my life.
You're joyfully neighing
just to be with him?
Laughter of flames
allures you to follow?
Feel how my bosom
so hotly burns.
Radiant fire
takes hold of my heart.
On to embrace him,
to live in his arms,
thus yoked to him ever
in mightiest love!
Heiajaho! Grane!
Give your lord greeting!

Heiaho! Grane!
Grüss' deinen Herren!

(*Sie hat sich auf das Ross geschwungen
und hebt es jetzt zum Sprung.*)

Siegfried! Siegfried! Sieh!
Selig grüsst dich dein Weib!

(*Sie sprengt das Ross mit einem Satz
in den brennenden Scheithaufen. So-
gleich steigt prasselnd der Brand hoch
auf, so dass das Feuer den ganzen
Raum vor der Halle erfüllt und diese
selbst schon zu ergreifen scheint. Entsetzt drängen sich die Männer und
Frauen nach dem Vordergrunde.
Plötzlich bricht das Feuer zusammen,
so dass nur noch eine düst're Glut-
wolke über der Stätte schwebt. Der
Rhein ist vom Ufer her mächtig
angeschwollen, und wälzt seine Flut
über die Brandstätte. Auf den Wogen
sind die drei Rheintöchter herbei-
geschwommen. Hagen, der seit dem
Vorgange mit dem Ringe in wachsender Angst Brünnhilde's Benehmen
beobachtet hat, gerät beim Anblicke
der Rheintöchter in höchsten
Schreck; er wirft hastig Speer, Schild
und Helm von sich, und stürzt wie
wahnsinnig sich in die Flut.*)

HAGEN

Zurück vom Ring!

(*Woglinde und Wellgunde umschlingen
mit ihren Armen seinen Nacken, und
ziehen ihn so mit sich in die Tiefe:
Flosshilde, ihnen voran, hält jubelnd
den gewonnenen Ring in die Höhe.
Am Himmel bricht zugleich von
fern her eine, dem Nordlicht ähnliche
rötliche Glut aus, die sich immer
weiter und stärker verbreitet. Von
dieser Helligkeit beleuchtet, sieht man
die drei Rheintöchter auf ruhigeren
Wellen des, allmählich wieder in sein
Bett zurückgetretenen, Rheines, lustig mit dem Ringe spielend, im Rei-
gen schwimmen. Aus den Trümmern
der zusammengestürzten Halle sehen
die Männer und Frauen, in höchster
Ergriffenheit, dem wachsenden Feuerschein am Himmel zu. Als dieser
endlich in lichtester Helligkeit leuchtet, erblickt man den Saal Walhall's,
in welchem die Götter und Helden
versammelt sitzen. Helle Flammen
scheinen in dem Saal der Götter auf-
zuschlagen.*)

DAS ENDE.

(She springs to the horse's back and raises him for a leap.)

Siegfried! Siegfried! See!
Brünnhilde hails you with joy!

(She urges the horse with one leap into the burning pyre. The fire blazes high, filling the entire space before the hall, which it seems about to devour. The men and women in terror crowd toward the extreme front. When all seems wrapped in flames the glow is suddenly extinguished so that only a cloud of smoke is seen which lies upon the horizon like a fogbank. At the same time the Rhine upswells mightly and pours its waters over the pyre. The three Rhine-maidens are riding the waves and appear by the pyre. Hagen, who has watched Brünnhilde's activities with increasing anxiety, is alarmed on the appearance of the Rhine daughters.

He flings away his spear, shield and helmet, and madly plunges into the flood, crying:)

HAGEN

The ring is mine!

(Voglinda and Vellgunda twine their arms round his neck and draw him below. Flosshilda holds up the recovered ring joyously. Through the cloud bank breaks an increasing red glow. In its light the Rhine is observed to have returned to its bed, and the girls are circling and playing with the ring on the calm water. From the ruins of the half-burnt hall the men and women perceive with awe the light in the sky, in which now appears the Hall of Valhalla, where the gods and heroes are seen sitting together. Bright flames seize on the abode of the gods.)

END OF THE OPERA